BLOOM

Photographed by Christopher Smith

BLOOM

Bill Chudziak, Jo Readman
& Anne Swithinbank

C&B

4

A CHANNEL FOUR BOOK

CONTENTS

INTRODUCTION

FLOWERS COME IN ALL SHAPES, sizes, colours and scents and, whether seen from afar or close to, are one of nature's greatest art forms. Blooms take us through the seasons, their ephemeral beauty delighting our senses year after year. They can be appreciated in the wild, grown to brighten up our homes and gardens and used to celebrate special events in our lives.

Mankind has had an intimate relationship with flowers for centuries, although initially flowering plants were grown for utility rather than for admiration. It has been suggested that in medieval times they were also given mystical importance with, for example, the lily standing for purity and the daisy for humility. In the 1500s flowering plants began to be grown for their beauty as well as their uses. Gardening became increasingly popular as people became more interested, and even obsessed, with growing flowers. The range of flowers began to expand, with the deliberate cultivation of unusual colour forms of native plants or of mutants such as doubles – which some foreigners attributed to the wet British climate! There were also introductions from abroad, including the first tulip, new irises and anemones. The era of organized plant hunting took this process a step further. In the seventeenth century the Tradescants brought back plants from Europe, Russia, North Africa, Virginia and the West Indies. Plant hunting grew in subsequent

LEFT
Helenium 'Wyndley'

RIGHT
Meconopsis grandis

centuries, as even more treasures were found in South Africa, Australia, North America, China and the Himalayas. With blue meconopsis from the Himalayas rubbing shoulders with lupins from North America, the world of flowers had entered the garden. Nurserymen, too, added to the mixture, breeding and hybridizing many garden plants to get improved performance such as larger and brighter blooms and stronger growth. The range of flowers available to the gardener grew at an incredible rate and is still expanding.

Yet flowers are not here to provide us with an ever-changing canvas; they have been flowering happily for over 65 million years. To humans they may signify beauty, purity and innocence, but they exist for one reason only ... reproduction.

Plants started life in the water. As they evolved to grow on land they became, essentially, immobile. Trapped, with their roots in the soil and their heads in the air, they needed a means of bringing about encounters between the male and female parts in order to reproduce. This often required a go-between that had to be attracted to the bloom, so many flowers became the beauties of the plant world. Their wonderful shapes and scents, brightly coloured petals, intricate arrangement of reproductive parts and hidden treasure troves of nectar evolved to bring about a perfect relationship with insects and other animals. They became messengers, carrying pollen (the flower's equivalent of sperm) from one plant to another. Flowers hold even more surprises when looked at through the eyes of pollinators such as bees, who can see into the ultraviolet part of the spectrum; to them, some yellow flowers are an enticing purple and some plain white flowers are overlaid

with bright purple lines radiating from the centre. These are nectar guides, or 'bee lines', and they act like road signs to direct the bee to the nectar and pollen.

The idea that flowers were reproductive organs, pollinated by insects, was not really accepted until the mid-seventeenth century; when it was first publicized it caused quite a stir. Many people regarded the concept as totally disgusting. We have now overcome some of our prejudices and can still admire flowers for their beauty, while also marvelling at their function.

The structure of a flower consists of compressed shoots with four whorls of modified leaves. These comprise the sepals, collectively called the calyx, which are usually leaf-like and green and protect and enclose the flower bud; the petals, collectively called the corolla, which are generally coloured, often perfumed and advertise the blooms to attract pollinators; the stamens, or male parts, consisting of pollen contained in anthers held on top of stalks called the filaments; and the carpel, or female parts. The receptive stigma at the tip of the carpel is joined to the ovary by a slender tube called the style. The ovary contains the all-important ovule or ovules (the eggs) awaiting the pollen to turn them into the seeds for the next generation. Some flowers have an intermediate structure that is a bit like a petal and a bit like a sepal; this is known as the tepal.

The overall aim is to get the pollen grains from the anther to land on the sticky stigma of the right sort of flower: pollen grains and stigma surfaces are like pieces of jigsaw, only the right grain will fit. Plants have spent centuries perfecting this process, which includes sending out complex chemical signals. Pollinators, such as bees, tend to be attracted to one sort of flower at a time. Orchids are an excellent example of the most amazing and specific relationships that plants have evolved with insects. *Angraecum sesquipedale*, an orchid from Madagascar, has a flower spur 30 cm (1 ft) long, with nectar at its base that can only be reached by one sort of moth, which has a tongue of exactly the same length.

Preferably, the pollen has to land on a different flower of the same species, to encourage some variety. The blooms have got this well organized, too. In some species, stamens and carpels in the same flower mature at different times, whereas in others they are positioned within the flowers in such a way that one cannot possibly reach the other, some have pollen that will not fit onto their own stigma and others play safe by having completely separate male and female flowers.

Flowers all belong to specific families. Like our own families, plants have distant and close relations, some live near each other while others may reside on the far side of the world. With some individuals, the family resemblances are difficult to fathom at first but on closer examination there is something about the flowers that shows they come from the same stable (see page 188).

In *Bloom* we delve into six very different but well-loved plant families, exploring the range of flowers and meeting the people who love to grow them. We bring you tips and advice on how to cultivate these plants, and discover some of the ways in which flowers have been used in the past and how they are used today. There are plants and flowers for the beginner, for the experienced gardener and the plantsperson as well as ideas for flower lovers who do not have a garden. Yet whatever the family, the relations or the name, the main reason for growing and using flowers is for pure pleasure. Enjoy.

SAYING IT WITH FLOWERS

From a singular rose to the red poppies of Remembrance Sunday, flowers are widely recognized as symbols of love, gratitude or condolence. They also have a centuries-old association with celebrations of fertility and the turning of the seasons.

WILD OR CULTIVATED, local or imported, flowers are part of our folklore. Although many of the rituals and customs associated with flowers originated hundreds of years ago, their popularity continues.

FLOWER CUSTOMS

One of the largest, most important of the old rural festivals was May Day, a celebration of the coming of summer with its attendant associations with fertility rites. Hawthorn is perhaps the most well known of the flowers used on this day, but a number of others had their part to play. Marsh marigold *(Caltha palustris)* was considered effective in warding off witches and fairies, particularly on the night of 30th April, May Eve, when they were believed to be at their most active and therefore dangerous. The act of 'maying' involved young people spending the night in the woods gathering flowers and branches and cutting down a tree for a maypole. These were brought back to the village on the morning of 1st May when the maypole was then erected, and elaborate garlands, hoops and crowns were made.

Early May was also host to a number of local festivals. Children celebrated Fraw Cup Sunday by bringing posies of wild fritillaries, *Fritillaria meleagris,* to villagers' cottage doors. This custom was local to the Thames valley, as this is where most of the country's fritillary meadows were (and still are) situated. Fraw Cup refers to one of the many common names given to this flower: crow cup, frog cup, snake's head and dead men's bells are just a selection.

Another ancient flower festival that is still celebrated to this day is known as Furry Day, which is enacted in Helston, Cornwall. On May 8th, the people of the town decorate doorways, shop fronts, streets (and themselves) with any flower available, mostly bluebells and lily-of-the-valley. Part of the festival is the 'Hal an Tow', a crop fertility ritual – part parade, part mumming play – that is performed with a number of set dances throughout the town.

Well dressing – decorating wells with flowers – is one of the most local popular folk traditions. Every year, more and more villages are participating.

The custom of well dressing probably began with the Celts, who were thought to have adorned wells with flowers and greenery in homage to revered water goddesses, whose images they carved onto headstones that marked the site of the

REMEMBER ME

Since the 1920s, the red poppy has come to symbolize remembrance of those who died in battle

well. Later, Christianity took over the custom; most of these wells and springs were rededicated to Christian saints and were then celebrated in accordance with the new religion.

The village of Tissington in Derbyshire has the longest documented tradition of well dressing. Legend has it that the purity of its spring water saved the people of the village from the plague in 1348-49; and that in 1615, a year of drought, the spring water there kept flowing even when that of the surrounding villages had dried up completely.

For a well dressing, flowers are torn apart and then reassembled into large floral pictures, which are placed next to the well. Flowers are collected from village gardens and nearby fields, and are chosen not only for their colour but also according to how long they will last – moon daisies and marguerites, for example, are a staple in the summer well dressings of Derbyshire. It takes days of painstaking work to push each flower petal into the soft clay in the frame, and the combined work-force of the whole village is needed to complete the picture. A church ceremony and village fête will usually open the well dressing officially, but the best time to be there is the night before. Then you will see the frantic finishing touches being made to the frames, before they are carried in triumph through the village to be erected at the well.

THE LANGUAGE OF FLOWERS

The idea of flowers being chosen to convey a specific message is thought to have originated in the East, namely from women in the Turkish harems. The 'language of flowers' spread to Europe, and became a craze in mid-1800s France. Later, Victorian Britain adopted the new flower language with enthusiasm. Always eager to find a veiled way of expressing sensuality, dictionaries of the hidden meaning of flowers became bestsellers, and even the way that blooms were placed in a bouquet could convey a different message of love. Sweet violets, for example, symbolized modesty, a rose meant true love and a white lily signified youthful innocence and purity.

An example of a more serious significance attached to a flower is the way in which red poppies have come to symbolize the countless dead in two world wars. In the last few years the sight of a glorious poppy field has become common again due to the EU encouraging farmers to let their fields lie fallow, and we may gradually return to the days when the poppy was seen as corn's natural companion. The Assyrians called it Daughter of the Field, the Greeks classed it as one of Aphrodite's flowers (she was the goddess of vegetation, among other things). The Romans thought it to be sacred to their corn goddess Ceres. That the flower was believed to be under the protection of the gods is perhaps reflected in the more recent superstitions surrounding it: picking it was thought to cause thunder, hence the common names thunderball, thundercup, and lightnings.

LOVES ME, LOVES ME NOT

The children's game of counting daisy petals was thought to answer the world's oldest question

11

THE
DAISY
FAMILY

Members of the daisy family come in all colours,
shapes and sizes, and are distributed throughout
the world, from the Arctic to the tropics.
Many have found a home in our gardens,
from gate-crashing weeds to invited,
beautiful herbaceous perennials.

COMPOSITAE

FLOWER FACTS

THE BIRDS AND THE BEES

❧

O F ALL THE FLOWERING plants in the world, over ten per cent belong to the daisy family. The size and success of this family may relate to the structure of their flowers. Each flowerhead (capitulum), at the top of the stalk, looks just like a single flower but is in fact composed of hundreds of tiny flowers – individually known as florets – hence the scientific name Compositae, meaning composed of separate parts. Acting just like a single flower, these flowerheads are very efficient, saving on stems and enabling an insect to pollinate many florets in one visit.

Take a look at some typical daisies: the tubular florets in the middle are known as the discs and the flat florets around the edge, which look like petals, are known as the rays. The rays are usually sterile and act to attract the attention of passing insects, the disc florets hold the reproductive equipment and get the insect's attention on arrival! There are several more floret shapes in the family. Dandelion flowerheads, for example, are made up of hundreds of 'ligulate' florets, which are bisexual and strap-shaped with five-toothed serrated tips.

Some of the fertile florets, which have male and female parts, consist of a cylinder of fused petals (a corolla tube) in which nestle five male stamens that are also fused to form a tiny goblet. The pollen falls into the base of this narrow goblet and is swept up to the outside world and awaiting insects by minuscule hairs on the sides of the female style as it grows up from the centre. Later the tip of the style opens out like the forked tongue of a snake to reveal its receptive stigma awaiting pollen from another flower. This excellent system is designed to encourage cross pollination, but if this does not succeed, all is not lost   the stigma bends back sufficiently to get pollen from its own floret.

Each fertilized floret produces a single, one-seeded fruit which often possesses a ring of hairs called the pappus, to aid dispersal, like the seeds of the familiar dandelion clock. Dispersal on the wind ensures that the hundreds of seeds produced from the one flowerhead spread far and wide, preventing competition for space and allowing the plants to colonize large areas.

Apart from the flower shape, other family traits include: leaves that are usually simple and opposite or alternate, and the presence of resin canals, and internal channels next to the plant's water vessels containing resin, a sticky insoluble chemical. One tribe, the Lactuceae, are a bit different and instead of resin canals have latex ducts. Dandelion is in this tribe, and milky latex can be seen when you break off a dandelion stalk. The latex from the Russian dandelion, *Taraxacum koksaghyz,* is even used in the production of rubber.

LEFT
GERBERA

WILD DAISIES

WILD DAISIES inhabit open ground, water margins, cliffs and even woodlands. Many are weeds of cultivation and some have found their way into our gardens. The range is enormous, so a few characteristic members have been chosen as representatives.

First and probably the most well known is the good old daisy, *Bellis perennis*, whose flowers appear from spring to late autumn, peaking in summer. An old proverb relates that when you put your foot on seven daisies, you know that summer has come. The name daisy originates from 'day's eye', as the flowers open in the day and close at night and in dull weather. 'Bellis' means beautiful, and many coloured and double forms of this species have been admired and cultivated since Elizabethan times. The less romantic name, bruisewort, is a reminder that daisies were once used in ointments to cure flesh wounds.

Coltsfoot (*Tussilago farfara*), although not so welcome in the garden, is renowned for its medicinal properties. *Tussis* is Latin for cough and *ago*, for action. The leaves were made into a tea or smoked as a cure for coughs and asthma. Despite being a pernicious weed, its sunshine yellow flowers are very attractive and they are sometimes called 'son before the father', appearing in spring before the large hoof-shaped leaves. A less attractive weed, groundsel (*Senecio vulgaris*) derives its name from the Anglo-Saxon *groundeswelge* or ground swallower. The annual plants produce over 1,000 seeds, each of which can travel long distances on the wind.

BELOW LEFT
DAISY
Bellis perennis

BELOW RIGHT
DANDELION
Taraxacum section *ruderalia*

When they land, they can germinate, grow and set seed in five weeks.

Tansy (*Tanacetum vulgare*), which grows wild in hedgerows and roadsides, is a welcome member of the herb garden. An attractive perennial with feathery leaves, its round, flat yellow flowers gave it the name buttons. The herb was used to flavour tansy cakes, eaten at Easter. The plant has also been used to dispel worms in children, as a green dye, and as a companion to fruit bushes to ward off pests.

Dandelions (*Taraxacum* sp.) are really useful plants: coffee is made from the roots, wine from the flowers, beer from the dried leaves, and salad from torn-up (not cut) young leaves, which can also be cooked like spinach. The name dandelion is from the French *dent de lion*, lion's teeth. An old name is 'wet the bed', in French *piss en lit*, as the plant is a strong diuretic. Yet another name, priest's crown, does not refer to the crown of florets but to the bald stalk which, after the seeds have flown, resembles a shorn head. The scientific name, *Taraxacum*, is from the Greek *taraxos*, disorder, and *akos*, remedy, and refers to the many medicinal uses of the plant. Dandelions have been used to treat liver complaints, help digestion and remove warts.

Not all dandelions are the same. There are over 70 species of the weed type, collectively known as *Taraxacum* section *ruderalia*. The plants make perfect tenacious weeds. They regenerate from pieces of chopped-up root, withstand drought, and spread far and wide using their parachute seeds. They can also reproduce without a partner or even fertilization. This means that the offspring should be identical, but the seeds can change their genes and chromosomes slightly to give a bit of variation. Dandelions also exhibit hybrid vigour, a little bit like an F1 flower, but one that can produce offspring that are just as vigorous as the parent.

Yet despite all this tough talk, the dandelion is not a very good competitor and is less common in the wild than in cultivated ground, where it makes full use of the conditions created for ornamentals.

Thistles are a type of daisy, too. The spear thistle (*Cirsium vulgare*) is biennial, completing its life cycle in two years. It has beautiful pinky purple flowerheads, but the prickly, sharp spines all over the plant make it an unwelcome border flower. The greater burdock (*Arctium lappa*), also closely related to the thistles, makes a tall, handsome biennial plant with heart-shaped leaves and purple flowers. Burdock seeds are surrounded by a coat of brown, hooked prickles and often take the opportunity to hitchhike on passers-by. The Latin name derives from '*arktos*', a bear (referring to the roughness of the burrs) and '*lappa*', to seize. As well as giving inventors the idea for Velcro®, burdock found its way onto our ancestors' tables. The cooked stems were prepared like asparagus, and eaten with caution – the plants are known to have mild laxative properties.

RIGHT
SPEAR THISTLE
Cirsium vulgare

WILD DAISIES

YARROW
Achillea millefolium

GREATER BURDOCK
Arctium lappa

MUGWORT
Artemisia vulgaris

DAISY
Bellis perennis

MUSK THISTLE
Carduus nutans

CARLINE THISTLE
Carlina vulgaris

BLACK KNAPWEED
Centaurea nigra

CHICORY
Cichorium intybus

CORN MARIGOLD
Chrysanthemum segetum

CREEPING THISTLE
Cirsium arvense

SMOOTH HAWKSBEARD
Crepis capillaris

HEMP AGRIMONY
Eupatorium cannabinum

COMMON CUDWEED
Filago vulgaris

BLUE LETTUCE
Lactuca perennis

NIPPLEWORT
Lapsana communis

COTTON THISTLE
Onopordum acanthium

COMMON FLEABANE
Pulicaria dysenterica

GROUNDSEL
Senecio vulgaris

TANSY
Tanacetum vulgare

DANDELION
Taraxacum section *ruderalia*

COLTSFOOT
Tussilago farfara

THE FLOWERING YEAR

With over 1,100 genera and 25,000 species, daisies are a real flower-feast. The main flush of garden daisies bloom from high summer to mid-autumn, but several add colour at other times of the year.

The first blooms are the thugs of the family: *Petasites fragrans*, the winter heliotrope, brighten up late winter with vanilla-scented, pinkish white clustered flowerheads. An invasive plant, it makes excellent ground cover and will tolerate shade and low temperates. Another early bloom is yellow coltsfoot *(Tussilago farfara)* and, although less welcome, its flowers are no less beautiful.

Doronicum, yellow leopard's bane, comes in many varieties from 25 cm (10 in) *D. orientale* 'Goldzwerg' to 90 cm (3 ft) *D. x excelsum* 'Harpur Crewe'. A close relative, *Inula acaulis*, provides another low-growing, yellow spring daisy.

The family's stunning architectural plants include celmisias, whose white flowers and silver leaves give year-round value, as do artemisias. Evergreen shrubby daisies include ozothamnus and olearia. *Olearia phlogopappa*, the Tasmanian daisy bush, is covered with bright blue flowers in May, followed by *Olearia macrodonta*, the New Zealand holly, with its broad panicles of white flowerheads in June.

APRIL

LEOPARD'S BANE
Doronicum orientale (HP)
April–June

INULA
Inula acaulis (HP)
April–May

DANDELION
Taraxacum section *ruderalia* (HP)
April–November

MAY

POT MARIGOLD
Calendula officinalis (HA)
May–October

NEW ZEALAND DAISY
Celmisia hookeri (HP)
May–July

GERBERA
Gerbera jamesonii (HHP)
May–August

TASMANIAN DAISY BUSH
Olearia phlogopappa (HS)
May

JUNE

YARROW
Achillea filipendulina 'Gold Plate' (HP)
June–September

ANTHEMIS
Anthemis tinctoria (HP)
June–September

SWAN RIVER DAISY
Brachyscome multifida (HHP)
June–September

MUSK THISTLE
Carduus nutans (HB)
June–September

CENTAURA
Centaurea macrocephala (HP)
June–July

TICKSEED
Coreopsis verticilliata (HP)
June–September

FLEABANE
Erigeron speciosus (HP)
June–August

BLUE MARGUERITE
Felicia amelloides (HHP grown as A)
June–August

BLANKET FLOWER
Gaillardia grandiflora (HP)
June–October

OSTEOSPERMUM
Osteospermum 'Pink Whirls' (HP)
June–October

COTTON LAVENDER
Santolina pinnata (HHPS)
June–August

FEBRUARY

WINTER HELIOTROPE
Petasites fragrans (HP)
February–March

COLTSFOOT
Tussilago farfara (HP)
February–April

MARCH

COMMON DAISY
Bellis perennis (HP)
March–October

JULY

AFRICAN DAISY
Arctotis x *hybrida* 'Flame'
(HHA)
July–October

MARGUERITE
Argyranthemum frutescens
'Mary Wootton' (HHP)
July–October

GLOBE ARTICHOKE
Cynara scolymus (HP)
July–September

PURPLE CONE FLOWER
Echinacea purpurea (HP)
July–September

GLOBE THISTLE
Echinops bannaticus (HP)
July–August

GAZANIA
Gazania x *hybrida* (HHP)
July–November

EVERLASTING FLOWER
Helichrysum bracteatum syn.
Bracteantha bracteatum (HHA)
July–September

GIANT INULA
Inula magnifica (HP)
July–September

LIGULARIA
Ligularia hodgsonii (HP)
July–August

CLIMBING GAZANIA
Mutisia oligodon (H/HHP)
July–October

SCOTCH THISTLE
Onopordum acanthium (HB)
July–August

CONE FLOWER
Rudbeckia fulgida
'Goldstrum' (HP)
July–September

GOLDEN ROD
Solidaster luteus (HP)
July–September

AFRICAN MARIGOLD
Tagetes erecta (HHA)
July–November

AUGUST

COSMEA
Cosmos bipinnatus (HHA)
August–September

DAHLIA
Dahlia 'Bishop of
Llandaff' (HHP)
August–November

SNEEZEWEED
Helenium autumnale (HP)
August–October

SEPTEMBER

MICHAELMAS DAISY
Aster 'Photograph' (HP)
September–October

CHRYSANTHEMUM
Dendranthema 'Shirley' (HP)
September–November

**WILLOW-LEAVED
SUNFLOWER**
Helianthus salicifolius (HP)
September–October

GAY FEATHER
Liatris spicata (HP)
September

From June to late summer, the firework show begins with blooms of all shapes, colours and sizes rising in quick succession. For the herbaceous border, try blue globe thistles, yellow achilleas, golden rod and ligularias for the back; dahlias, coreopsis, anthemis, and heleniums for the centre; and for the front, multi-coloured osteospermums, erigerons, gaillardias and gazanias. Annual chrysanthemums, pot marigolds and cosmeas sown in spring provide a palette of colour the same year, and tender annuals and perennials such as felicias, brachyscome and argyranthemums make effective displays in containers.

Late autumn sees towering helianthus, the perennial sunflowers, forming a sunshine backdrop to a border fronted by rainbows of dahlias followed by clouds of purple and pink asters. Chrysanthemums (now dendranthemas) give the last blast in the borders. At the front are Japanese poms such as *Dendranthema* 'Bronze Elegance'. Behind, taller Rubellum and Korean strains of hardy chrysanthemums can go right into the first frosts.

NOVEMBER

CINERARIA
Senecio x *hybridus* syn. *Cineraria*
x *hybrida* (HHP)
November–March

KEY
A: annual B: biennial P: perennial S: shrub
HH: half-hardy H: hardy T: tree

DAISY DIRECTORY

TYPE OF PLANT	(H) HEIGHT (S) SPREAD	CONDITIONS REQUIRED (SEE KEY)	PLANT TYPE AND CULTIVATION TIP	PROPAGATION
Achillea filipendulina 'Gold Plate'	**H** 1.2 m (4 ft) **S** 75 cm (30 in)	◐☼✹✹✹	Evergreen perennial. Dead head for more blooms.	Lift, divide and replant in spring.
Anthemis tinctoria 'Wargrave'	**H** 75 cm (30 in) **S** 75 cm (30 in)	◐☼✹✹✹	Evergreen perennial. Cut back untidy growth in autumn.	Lift, divide and replant in spring or autumn. Take basal cuttings in spring.
ASTER *Aster* 'Climax'	**H** 1.8 m (6 ft) **S** 60 cm (2 ft)	◐☼◑✹✹✹	Deciduous perennial. Must be well grown to withstand mildew.	Lift, divide and replant in spring.
Aster x *frikartii*	**H** 75 cm (30 in) **S** 60 cm (2 ft)	◐☼✹✹✹	Deciduous perennial. Requires staking.	Lift, divide and replant in spring. Basal cuttings in spring.
Calendula officinalis	**H** 60 cm (2 ft) **S** 30-60 cm (1-2 ft)	◐☼✹✹✹	Annual. Dead head regularly.	Seed.
Carduus nutans	**H** 1.2–1.5 m (4–5 ft) **S** 1.8 m (6 ft)	◐☼✹✹✹	Biennial. Pull up excess seedings.	Seed.
Celmisia hookeri	**H** 45 cm (18 in) **S** 45 cm (18 in)	◐☼◑✹✹✹	Alpine perennial. Difficult in hot, dry climates.	Seed and rarely cuttings.
Centaurea macrocephala, *C.* 'Pulchra Major'	**H** 90 cm (3 ft) **S** 90 cm (3 ft)	◐☼✹✹✹	Herbaceous perennial. Tidy up in winter.	Seed. Division in spring.
Dahlia 'Bishop of Llandaff'	**H** 1.2 m (4 ft) **S** 90 cm (3 ft)	◐☼✹	Tender tuberous perennial. Lift and store frost free in winter.	Basal cuttings in early spring.
Echinacea purpurea	**H** 1.2 m (4 ft) **S** 1.2 m (4 ft)	◐☼✹✹✹	Herbaceous perennial. Cut back after flowering.	Seed and division.
Echinops bannaticus 'Taplow Blue'	**H** 1.5 m (5 ft) **S** 60 cm (2 ft)	◐☼◑✹✹✹	Deciduous. Requires staking.	Division in autumn. Seed in autumn. Root cuttings in winter.

Gerbera jamesonii	**H** 60 cm (2 ft) **S** 45 cm (18in)	○ ☀ ☀	*Half-hardy perennial.* *Likes light, sandy soil.*	*Heel cuttings from* *side shoots.*
HELIANTHUS *Helianthus atrorubens*	**H** 1.8 m (6 ft) **S** 1.8 m (6 ft)	○ ☀ ☀ ☀ ☀	*Herbaceous perennial.* *Requires staking.*	*Division of creeping* *rootstock.*
Helianthus salicifolius	**H** 2.5 m (8 ft) **S** 90 cm (3 ft)	○ ☀ ☀ ☀ ☀	*Deciduous perennial.* *Requires staking.* *Spreads at the root.*	*Lift, divide and replant in* *spring or autumn. Basal* *cuttings in spring.*

HELENIUM
    Helenium 'Crimson Beauty'
    H. 'Wyndley', H. 'Butterpat'
	H 1.2 m (4 ft)
	S 60 cm (2 ft)
		○ ☀ ☀ ☀ ☀	*Deciduous perennial.*
			Water during drought.
			Requires staking.
				Lift, divide and replant
				in spring or autumn.
				Basal cuttings in spring.

HELICHRYSUM
    Helichrysum bracteatum 'Dargan Hill
    Monarch' *(syn. Bracteantha bracteata),*
    H. b. 'Silver Bush', *H. b.* 'Skynet'
	H 60 cm (2 ft)
	S 45 cm (18 in)
		○ ☀ ☀	*Evergreen.*
			Shelter from frost.
			Prune mature plants
			in spring.
				Named varieties can be
				propagated by shoot-tip
				cuttings in spring and
				early summer.

Inula magnifica	**H** 2.5 m (8 ft) **S** 90 cm (3 ft)	○ ☀ ☀ ☀ ☀	*Herbaceous perennial.* *Requires staking.*	*Seed and division.*
Liatris spicata	**H** 90 cm (3 ft) **S** 1.2 m (4 ft)	○ ☀ ☀ ☀ ☀	*Herbaceous perennial.* *Cut back after* *flowering.*	*Seed and division.*
LIGULARIA *Ligularia hodgsonii*	**H** 90 cm (3 ft) **S** 90 cm (3 ft)	◐ ☀ ◑ ☀ ☀ ☀	*Deciduous perennial.* *Requires stake. Protect* *from slugs.*	*Lift, divide and replant* *in spring or autumn.*
Ligularia 'Wiehenstephan'	**H** 90 cm (3 ft) **S** 60 cm (2 ft)	◐ ☀ ◑ ☀ ☀ ☀	*Deciduous perennial.* *Protect from slugs.*	*Lift, divide and replant* *in spring or autumn.*
Mutisia oligodon	**H** 1.2 m (4 ft) **S** 90 cm (3 ft)	○ ☀ ◑ ☀ ☀	*Evergreen perennial.* *Seed in spring.* *Layer in autumn.*	*Seed.*
Olearia phlogopappa 'Comber's Blue'	**H** 1.8 m (6 ft) **S** 1.8 m (6 ft)	○ ☀ ☀	*Evergreen shrub.* *Tolerates light, sandy* *soil.*	*Semi-ripe cuttings* *in summer.*
Santolina pinnata ssp. *neapolitana* 'Edward Bowles'	**H** 60 cm (2 ft) **S** 90 cm (3 ft)	○ ☀ ☀ ☀ ☀	*Evergreen perennial.* *Shear back in spring* *to retain neat shape.*	*Semi-ripe cuttings* *in summer.*

KEY
○ Well drained soil ◐ Moist soil ● Wet soil ☀ Sun ◑ Partial shade ☀ Tolerates full shade
☀ Half-hardy to 0°C (32°F) ☀☀ Frost-hardy to –5°C (23°F) ☀☀☀ Fully hardy to –15°C (5°F)

THE GARDENS
RHS ROSEMOOR

One of the best gardens at which to admire members of the vast daisy family and learn how they can be used is RHS Rosemoor near Torrington in North Devon. To see the composites in their full glory, Anne Swithinbank made two trips there, once in sizzling midsummer and again on a wild autumnal day.

ROSEMOOR HAS AN interesting history and is a fascinating blend of old and new. In 1988 Lady Anne Berry (then Palmer) made a gift to the Royal Horticultural Society (RHS) of her house and existing 3.5 hectare (eight acre) garden, along with a further 13 hectares (32 acres) which had previously been pastureland. The RHS set about commissioning designs to transform the fields into a new garden, inspired by the fact that the heavy clay soil and higher rainfall would provide a very different growing environment to the dry, sandy, acid soil at their long established garden in Wisley, Surrey.

Christopher Bailes has been working at the garden since the RHS took control, initially with Jeremy Rougier, who was the Director for the first six years of the project. With their staff, they carefully nurtured bare fields into the beautiful gardens that we now see today.

On my summer visit, Chris and I toured the Spiral Garden, where the pale daisies of *Anthemis tinctoria* 'Wargrave' shone above stems of ferny foliage some 75

LEFT
COTTAGE AT ROSEMOOR

RIGHT
DYER'S CHAMOMILE
Anthemis tinctoria 'Wargrave'

cm (30 in) tall. 'Members of the daisy family are widely used here for both structure and summer colour,' said Chris. Anthemis have a classic, daisy-shaped flower head with an outer ring of ray florets surrounding an inner circle of disc florets. 'They flower for many weeks in summer,' Chris continued, 'but retain some leaves during winter, so we only trim them back in the autumn, finally cutting them right down in spring just before new growth starts.'

Strong foliage is important, illustrated by the silvery-leaved artemisias and pretty cotton lavender *Santolina pinnata* ssp. *neapolitana* 'Edward Bowles', which is blessed with both low mounds of fine silvery leaves and pale, creamy lemon button-shaped flowerheads.

Within the Compositae the varying shapes of the flowerheads are used to great structural effect. Healthy clumps of *Achillea filipendulina* 'Gold Plate' provide 1.2 m (4 ft) tall masses of fern-like foliage below the plate-like heads of golden flowers, which seem to hover like flying saucers. By contrast, the tiny blue flowers of globe thistle *Echinops bannaticus* 'Taplow Blue' are packed into orbs at the tops of sturdy 1.5 m (5 ft) tall stems.

'The soil here is a retentive, silty clay loam over clay with rock,' explained Chris. 'Combine this with a heavy rainfall and you can imagine the difficulties we've had. When I first arrived, I walked out to the square field and dug some trial pits to look at the soil profile. After lunch, my heart sank when I returned to find that my pits had filled with water, and this was only autumn.' So how did they sort this tricky site out? 'There was a lot of draining and levelling to do before we could implement the designs for the new gardens.'

ABOVE
YARROW
Achillea filipendulina
'Gold Plate'

RIGHT
GLOBE THISTLE
Echinops bannaticus
'Taplow Blue'

FAR RIGHT
COTTON LAVENDER
Santolina pinnata ssp.
neapolitana 'Edward
Bowles'

24

When you are the curator of an important, young and developing garden with thousands of RHS members and visitors watching your every move, you just have to get it right. 'Yes, I did feel as if the eyes of the world were upon me,' said Chris. 'Creating a major national garden from scratch certainly concentrates the mind.' Now that the clay has been tamed, it is remarkably fertile and most plants seem to thrive in it.

Creating borders based on the hotter colours of the spectrum is a popular design idea used in both public and private gardens. At Rosemoor, the Square Garden is a fine example. Heleniums star here, with their prominent, cone-shaped centres packed full of disc florets which are usually brown in bud, but turn yellow as the tiny flowers open from the outside of the cone, revealing their pollen. The outer ray florets can be yellow, red or bronze.

Pausing to admire a splendid clump of *Helenium* 'Crimson Beauty' towards the back of one of these hot beds, Chris and I talked about their natural habitat. 'In common with many other perennial daisies, they come from North America, in

this case from rather damp meadows or the edges of woods,' he explained. I could imagine whole areas of them swaying in amongst grasses. 'On our moisture-retentive and heavily mulched soil, it is not necessary to water regularly during average summers,' said Chris. 'We do step in during prolonged drought, targeting moisture-lovers like ligularia.'

Ligularias are partly responsible for the intense yellow and orange colours repeated throughout the square garden. Japanese *L. hodgsonii* bears 5 cm (2 in) wide flowerheads on plants 90 cm (3 ft) tall, while *L.* 'Weihenstephan' is grown for its spikes of yellow flowers.

I love to visit gardens during autumn, possibly because there is a sense of time being precious. On my return to Rosemoor, the weather could not have been more different and the autumnal plantings were dramatically lit by low shafts of sun, which alternated with short sharp showers as the wind swept rainclouds across the sky. 'Typical Devon weather,' commented Chris. 'It's quite normal for the rain to come at you sideways here.'

The blooms we had admired a few months earlier had faded and died, to be replaced by huge groups of Michaelmas daisies making soft clouds of flower. Repetition works well in flower beds, amply illustrated by several clumps of blue-flowered *Aster* 'Climax', which reaches 1.8 m (6 ft). *Aster novi-belgii* and its varieties are notorious mildew sufferers, but Rosemoor's plants were vigorous and healthy. 'There is a little bit of mildew if you look closely,' said Chris, 'but if the plants are grown well, they are rarely bothered by it.' Left to struggle on poor, sandy soil, they can be devastated by this disease. White powdery patches appear on the leaves, which, in extreme cases, turn brown and shrivel.

The solution to bad mildew problems is either to spray regularly with a fungicide, or better still, to grow resistant varieties. One of these is 75 cm (30 in)

LEFT
SNEEZEWEED
Helenium 'Crimson Beauty'

BELOW
Ligularia hodgsonii

BELOW RIGHT
Ligularia 'Wiehenstephan'

tall *Aster* x *frikartii*, whose flowers are characterized by their long elegant petals. 'These are in flower for three months from summer into autumn and look good growing with other plants, such as buddleia,' said Chris. The many different varieties of the New England aster (*A. novae-angliae*) and Italian starwort (*A. amellus*) also show good resistance to mildew.

Fitting in well with the silvery, soft-coloured theme of the garden were billowing clumps of 1.8–2.2 m (6–7 ft) tall *Aster* 'Photograph'. Masses of tiny pale flowers combined to give a cloud-like effect. This type does suffer from mildew, but again, this has been overcome by strength and vigour. I had heard some gardeners say that most Michaelmas daisies (*Aster amellus* is an exception) should be lifted, divided and replanted every year, but this made Chris laugh. 'We would not be able to find the time to do that. Besides which, I believe the plants need to reach their third year before their full potential is reached. Then they can be divided in spring and replanted before clumps become old and congested. We plant 17-20 fresh divisions 30 cm (1 ft) apart to form a good clump.'

FAR LEFT
**MICHAELMAS
DAISY**
Aster 'Climax'

LEFT
Aster x *frikartii*
'Mönch'

RIGHT
**WILLOW-LEAVED
SUNFLOWER**
Helianthus salicifolius

Another group of daisies guaranteed to bring freshness to the autumnal garden are chrysanthemums, though these days more accurately called *Dendranthema*. To see an example of a hardy dendranthema that would not take up too much space in a small garden, we strolled into the Square Garden to admire *D.* 'Nantyderry Sunshine'. This grows into a rounded bush 76 cm (30 in) high, smothered in clear, yellow flowers. In the world of dendranthemas, new varieties often occur through sporting, which is when a whole shoot of a plant undergoes a genetic change and suddenly produces flowers that are a different colour to the rest of the plant. Cuttings rooted from this portion will retain the different colour and can become a new variety. 'Nantyderry Sunshine' was one of several sports derived from a purple-pink variety called 'Mei-Kyo', brought into the country from Japan some 40 years ago.

As the sun went down we admired the last light just catching the petals of willow-leaved sunflower, *Helianthus salicifolius*. This plant reaches 2.5 m (8 ft), and made a large clump of swaying stems, brightening a quiet part of the garden with its golden yellow flowers.

The important point about all these plants from the Compositae family is that they are easy to grow and can be slotted in between shrubs and other herbaceous perennials. They are hardy, reliable and, although in some cases they die back in winter, new growth will appear in the spring. Plants can be easily rejuvenated and propagated by lifting the roots, dividing the clumps and replanting them during the autumn or in spring. Rooted shoots can be prised from the bases of dendranthemas, but they are more often propagated by early spring cuttings.

HILEYS' TENDER PERENNIALS

Brian and Heather Hiley who run their nursery in Wallington, near Croydon in Surrey, must surely be king and queen of the tender perennials. Gardeners look forward to their exhibits every year, where their high standards have won many RHS Gold Medals. Anne Swithinbank visited them to see their tender perennial daisies.

H ILEYS' NURSERY IS SITED in a unique open space. 'This was an area of small holdings which the local councils were obliged to buy after the First World War,' explained Heather. 'Lloyd George came up with the 'homes fit for heroes' scheme, by which lower-ranking officers returning from the War could rent out small market gardens. It sounds like a good idea, but it didn't really work because the councils could only afford poor land. Our plot, which we took on back in 1974, has only some 45 cm (18 in) of topsoil over chalk, and it's one of the best.'

The state of the soil is largely irrelevant now, since most of the Hiley's stock is confined to pots. A reminder of the old market garden days is an ancient delivery bike, now undergoing a second lease of life as a plant container. In honour of my visit, its basket was planted solely with daisies. Marguerites are firm favourites with the container *cognoscenti* and here, white-flowered *Argyranthemum frutescens* and double pink, anemone-centred *A.* 'Vancouver' gave shrubby height to the back.

LEFT
AN UNUSUAL CONTAINER

RIGHT
THE HILEYS' NURSERY

At the front arctotis, *Gazania* 'Christopher' and blue kingfisher daisy *Felicia* 'Astrid Thomas' were set off by three helichrysums, grown for their foliage. The soft variegated leaves of trailing *Helichrysum petiolare* 'Variegatum' and neater *H. p.* 'Roundabout' contrasted with hardy, silver *H. splendidum*.

Clustered outdoors in summer are hundreds of beautiful stock and display plants growing in large pots. Brian showed me some first-rate varieties of silvery-leaved *Bracteantha bracteata* (formerly *Helichrysum bracteatum*). This Australian scrubland plant has flowers with crisp straw-like petals and reaches 60 cm (2 ft) in height. I would definitely find room in my garden for golden yellow *B. b.* 'Dargan Hill Monarch', creamy white 'Skynet' or yellow-centred, white 'Silver Bush'.

Other Antipodean daisies include *Brachyscome multifida*, with blue ray florets and yellow disc florets. The Hileys also grow pink-flowered, coarse-leaved

LEFT
EVERLASTING FLOWER
Bracteantha bracteata 'Dargan Hill Monarch' (yellow) and 'Silver Bush' (white)

RIGHT
THE HILEYS' NURSERY

B. 'Strawberry Mousse', and the even more choice *B.* 'Harmony', which has a winning combination of dark stems and intense purple-blue flowers. Plants are potted on until each fills its own 30 cm (1 ft) diameter pot. Good compost with added slow-release fertilizer, adequate water and a weekly liquid feed ensure that they reach a height and spread of some 45 cm (18 in).

South African osteospermums are often called rain daisies, as their flowers typically open after wet weather. The outer ray florets of *O.* 'Pink Whirls' are nipped in halfway along their length, and change from pink to white towards the base. The contrasting disc florets are blue with orange pollen. New *O.* 'Zulu' is rich yellow with a bronze stripe along the back of each petal. Arctotis, the South African monarch of the veldt, change colour as they age. *A.* x *hybrida* 'Wine' starts off a deep pink, but fades to a paler shade; similarly, *A. h.* 'Flame' turns from rich orange to light orange. When many plants are grown together, the overall effect is shimmeringly beautiful.

Watering this massive collection of potted plants must take ages on a hot day. 'It does,' said Brian, 'and our water pressure crisis means starting at 5am.' However, gardeners with only a few larger containers should not find watering too onerous.

As Brian showed me his plants, I began to appreciate the value of studying them closely. By their very nature, the flowerheads of composites deserve this as they are so complex and beautifully coloured. Gazanias, particularly, had me transfixed and they certainly deserve a revival.

PLANTSMAN'S CHOICE

BILL CHUDZIAK

LIATRIS

At first, or even second glance, few people would pigeonhole liatris in the daisy family. *Liatris spicata*, by far the most common, is regularly available in garden centres or as sad specimens sold in plastic bags in supermarkets. It has narrow, dark-green leaves which continue up the somewhat stiff stems to where the flower spike begins. These spikes comprise a dense cluster of downy flowers, which are as soft and hazy as swansdown.

Typically, the colouring is an uncompromising violet-mauve, a shade which I love in some plants, like airy *Verbena bonariensis*, but find indigestable in others, like *Liatris spicata*. Habit of growth is the reason. Liatris are unusual in opening their flowers from the top of the spike downwards and this, to my mind, gives the flowerheads a top-heavy, dumpy look. They suggest the padded ramrods with which gunners used to load cannons. The white form, especially 'Floristan', is attractive and easier to place in the garden. They are showy and useful plants, however, flowering lengthily from midsummer onwards, so ignore my ill-natured remarks, and make your own judgements. Liatris is called blazing star or Kansas gay feather in its native America, where it grows on the prairie, as well

LEFT
GAY FEATHER *Liatris spicata*

as along highways and railroad tracks. Much more attractive and refined is the lovely *Liatris aspera* from the eastern USA. It has the same mauve colouring and downy petals, but individual flowers are placed apart on the spike, revealing incurved papery bracts. They remind me of floaty sea anemones. The plant is taller and less stiff, too, so the overall effect is interesting and elegant. A humus-rich soil in sun suits all liatris, and this one certainly merits a choice position. There are other liatris, all good garden plants, so if you like them, and can find them, try them all.

CELMISIA

Celmisias upset all our preconceptions about silver-leaved plants. We are apt to think of such plants as hailing from baked, impoverished scrubland, but these aristocratic daisies originate in the cloud-cooled meadows of New Zealand's mountainous South Island. *Celmisia hookeri* forms great architectural rosettes of stiff foliage which looks like hammered aluminium. In the best forms both upper and lower leaf surfaces are clad in an overcoat of silver or bronze hairs. From deep in the rosettes, in midsummer, emerge scaly silver stems topped by somewhat sinister-looking metallic buds. These open into surprisingly pretty daisy flowers, a showy 10 cm (4 in) across, with a thick ruff of bright white ray florets, and a central boss of yellow disc florets.

Celmisia hookeri

Olearia phlogopappa 'Comber's Blue'

Celmisia webbiae

POT MARIGOLD
Calendula officinalis

MUSK THISTLE
Carduus nutans

Centaurea macrocephala

Despite their size and robustness, these flowers are held jauntily upright on stems that look almost muscular. No quiet and subtle charmer, this plant booms 'Look at me. I dominate any company.' And so it does, for in this country it must grow among the small treasures of the rock garden to emulate life on the irrigated scree. Sharp drainage stops crown rot, but summer moisture replicates to some degree the snow-melt below the rock debris of its native sub-alpine home. Summer heat is anathema, so it flourishes in the cooler northern counties, Scotland, or, above all in the marvellous gardens of Ireland. 'David Shackleton', a gleaming silver cultivar from Ireland, is the crème de la crème.

Celmisia webbiae is smaller and shrubbier. The leaves, pine-green above but white below, have a pronounced silver midrib. They are resinously sticky, coating the fingers with a gummy substance. Propagate from division, fresh seed, or, in the case of *Celmisia webbii*, cuttings. If they like you, though, celmisias will proliferate, and a well-grown colony of this splendid daisy gives a rock garden enormous distinction.

OLEARIA

Most gardeners know the old favourite *Senecio* 'Sunshine' with its felty white leaves and corymbs of brassy daisies, but less familiar are the olearias, the daisy-bushes. Both of these shrubby Compositae hail from Australasia and they have been around our gardens for 150 years or more. They are supreme shrubs for coastal areas where they are in their element, and there is no better subject for planting in a windy salt-lashed seaside garden. In mild west-coast gardens olearias reach an enormous size, and they are robust enough to be planted as a windbreak.

Most commonly seen is *Olearia macrodonta* with shiny aqueous green leaves and a rather over-exuberant display of jolly white daisies. *Olearia phlogopappa* 'Comber's Blue' is a much more rarefied shrub, and deserves a choice and sheltered spot. The leaves of the plant are small and aromatic and the undersides and stems are coated with white felt. The flowers, borne in generous loose panicles, are of a strong violet-blue.

When these shrubs first appeared at the Chelsea Flower Show in 1930, exhibitors were adversely criticized for showing forced Michaelmas daisies in early summer. Indeed they uncannily resemble tall Michaelmas daisies, though, of course, lacking the rather prosaic leaves of the herbaceous plant. Despite this unpropitious debut, the plant went on to be awarded the accolade of an RHS First-class Certificate. Lacking the wind tolerance of its more robust cousins, 'Comber's Blue' is still happier in milder gardens where hard frosts are rare. Shelter and sharp drainage are essential. As it stays fairly compact it is ideal for a small garden or as part of a mixed border planting. The most splendid olearia, however, is 'Henry Travers', with narrow silver-backed leaves and immense flowers of rich lilac, purple-centred. If you have a warm garden, spare no effort to obtain this plant.

CALENDULA OFFICINALIS

Grow pot marigolds in your garden, and you will establish a link in a gardening chain that goes back seven hundred years or more. Botanically, they are *Calendula officinalis*, in cultivation for so long that no one is exactly sure of their wild origins. *Calendulas* are cheerful annuals, perfect for adding period charm and a splash of colour to an old-fashioned herb garden. For authenticity such plantings should be close to the old-fashioned single type, but as an ingredient in cottage-style borders, the range can be wider. By the sixteenth century there were many ornamental forms, doubles, pale forms and even a 'hen-and-chickens', which has small secondary flowers appearing from the main flowerhead. Modern seed strains have given us some attractive colour variations from cream to mahogany. 'Art Shades' is good and reliable. A March sowing in fertile soil and sun should bloom by May, and succession sowing will give flowers all summer, should you want them.

THISTLES

Most gardeners wage a war of attrition against thistles. A few, however, make excellent garden plants and their angular habit often makes a useful exclamation mark in contrast to a billowy summer planting. *Carduus nutans*, the musk thistle, is a British native, growing in poor and stony places mostly in the southern half of the country. It is a tall plant, reaching, perhaps, 1.2–1.5 m (4-5 ft) with wide branching heads and nodding purplish crimson flowers, which have a discernible musky scent. The whole plant is protected by an armoury of vicious spines. You might use this plant in a hot dry gravel border, but you would always run the risk of busybodies pointing out deficiencies in your weeding. In any case, you would be wise to collect and remove the seed heads as it is a profligate self-seeder. It is, perhaps, one of those marginal garden plants that needs to be grown and placed with great conviction if it is to look intentional.

No such problem would exist with *Onopordum acanthium*. This is a giant of a plant, and a wonderful architectural accent. If suited it will reach 2.5 m (8 ft) and is interesting at each stage of its biennial lifespan. From a beefy silver seedling it matures into a vast rosette 90 cm (3 ft) across, which lasts through the winter. In its second year it throws up from the centre a stout winged stem of pewter grey, each ascending leaf larger than the last. Finally, it branches into a huge gaunt candelabrum of flowering stems. Having flowered, it dies, but even then it makes a handsome corpse, and the skeleton, if left, provides both autumn food and gymnasium activity for hosts

ABOVE
Centaurea 'Pulchra Major'

of goldfinches. Birds take most of the seed, but there are always one or two seedlings to ensure a succession, and they are so singularly recognizable that they are easily tweaked out if unwanted. Like most Compositae it seems reluctant to germinate in a seed tray, preferring to self-sow. In some warmer parts of the world it is a pernicious weed, and import of seed is forbidden. We do not find it a pest, and especially love to see its pale gothic form looming wanly over old roses at dusk.

Onopordum come from the Caucasus, a region that seems to specialize in coarsely splendid herbaceous plants. From the same area comes *Centaurea macrocephala*, a handsome plant for all sorts of situations. Robust enough to tolerate wild or problem areas, it even puts up with competition from tree roots. The fluffy yellow knapweed flowers emerge from dry papery bracts netted with darker veins, and they dry well if cut and hung upside down before the flowers open. In its native sub-alpine meadows it grows alongside *Geranium* x *magnificum*, a fantastic combination for a low-maintenance area of garden.

Much more refined is *Centaurea* 'Pulchra Major'. It takes a couple of years to settle down, but then forms a clump of dark grey jagged leaves with white felty undersides. The flowers, also encased in papery bracts, are composed of lots of individual florets of hot pink. It flowers for ages in midsummer, and is a useful border plant, almost as good in foliage as in flower. It originates from the eastern Mediterranean where it grows on light sandy soil, even on dunes, so a warm well-drained spot is essential. These and other ornamental thistles are distinct from anything else we grow in our borders. Their stateliness of form gives edge to soft-centred summer plantings, giving structure and style to cluttered or over-pretty borders. They are, above all, plants with personality.

ECHINACEA PURPUREA

This is one of the robust and good-looking daisies from North America that light up our gardens from midsummer to the frosts. What they lack in refinement, they make up for in panache, being, for the most part, stately and full of character. *Echinacea purpurea* throws up stout stems punctuated with rather undistinguished dark green leaves. At about 1.2 m (4 ft), the stems branch and terminate in a series of large handsome daisy-flowers. When fully open, the outer ray florets reflex sharply from the blunt-nosed central boss to form a flower that is shaped just like a shuttlecock. But the best thing about this daisy is the colour. The outer ray florets are an unusual and very distinct rosy mauve, the colour of a good fruity raspberry fool, and the inner florets which make up the centre are orange-brown, an unlikely but exciting colour combination.

There are some excellent cultivars, and the best of these keep the rare and lovely colouring of the type more or less unaltered. 'Robert Bloom' actually surpasses the original, being darker and richer in tone, blackcurrant rather than raspberry. 'Magnus' is a form with enormous flowers, and a maroon central boss – very striking. All are well worth growing and are lovely with other late border plants, sugar-pink sidalceas, for instance, or blue agapanthus. The white forms are somewhat more commonplace but nevertheless earn their place in the garden by virtue of their interesting flower shape and size. They have an ornithological air, as if the white shuttlecocks were about to launch themselves on the wing. 'White Lustre' or 'White Star' are the ones to look for.

These giant North American daisies – *Echinacea, Rudbeckia, Helianthus* and *Helianthella* – pack a great punch and are due for a revival. A deep rich soil in full sun best replicates their native habitat.

MUTISIA OLIGODON

These evergreen climbing daisies are the aristocrats of the compositae. *Mutisia oligodon* was introduced in the 1920s from the Andes, but although it has been in cultivation for 70 years, it remains rare and desirable. It is, more accurately, a scrambler rather than a climber. Seldom exceeding 1.2 m (4 ft), its thin stems and the wiry tendrils which tip every leaf give it an air of languid fragility. This plant is at its best hoisting itself over a small twiggy shrub where its rather untidy habit of growth is less apparent than in more formal positions.

The leaves are dark green with shallow-toothed edges which give the plant its specific epithet ('oligodon' means few-toothed), each with its terminal tendril. The flowers are wonderful, generous daisies, reminiscent of gazanias. The outer ray-florets, clear pink, are delicately fluted and taper elegantly inwards to the yellow central disc florets. The entire flower is arrestingly beautiful.

Despite the fact that everyone finds mutisias captivating, they remain rare in gardens. Not reliably hardy, they tend to predominate in the warmer areas of the country. Nevertheless, most gardens have microclimates where borderline plants can be risked, and *Mutisia oligodon* merits the choicest position.

Mutisias are difficult to acquire, though nurserymen who specialize in unusual climbers often offer several. Seed exchanges can provide seed, especially of mauvey pink *Mutisia ilicifolia*, equally lovely though reputedly not so hardy. *Mutisia decurrens*, with large reflexed orange daisies, is also desirable.

Established mutisias sucker freely from the base, but do not detach these as the plant detests root disturbance. In the wild the roots stay cool and damp amongst boulders, whilst the top-growth basks on sun-drenched rocks, so try to replicate these conditions.

RIGHT

PURPLE CONE FLOWER *Echinacea purpurea*

ABOVE
Mutisia oligodon

Gardeners with imagination and a few tricks up their sleeves ought to be able to succeed with these lovely plants.

INULA MAGNIFICA

This stately giant from the Caucasus is for those with large gardens: this plant needs elbow-room. Nor is it for gardeners with delicate sensibilities whose joy lies in nurturing little treasures. *Inula magnifica* is big, bold, beautiful and splendidly coarse. It starts the year by producing a mound of 90 cm (3 ft) long rough leaves. As the summer progresses, great stout stems rocket up to 2.5 m (8 ft), finally terminating in heads of brown buds. These open into large fine-rayed daisies, each 15 cm (6 in) across, and of a somewhat brassy yellow. The plant has enormous presence, and should always be planted where its theatricality can be appreciated – in front of shrubs (especially purple-leafed ones), or as an architectural feature of a wild or bog garden. Beside water is perfect. Ideally it should be viewed in its entirety to savour its splendour from top-to-toe.

Inula magnifica is easy to grow anywhere in Britain, being extremely hardy and undemanding as to sun or shade. It sulks in dry soil, however, and is at its spectacular best in damp, deep conditions. *Inula royleana,* from the Himalayas, reaches about 60 cm (2 ft), and produces large orange-yellow daisies with long, needle-fine rays. It is a classy plant, a consolation prize for northern gardeners who struggle with warm climate daisies, as it relishes cool moist air. It takes a couple of years to settle down, but matures into a star of the July garden. Its wonderful buds are like mathematical constructions, and the flowers unwind as they open, having been stored away like furled umbrellas.

Inula helenium, the elecampane, is a British native, in our gardens for centuries. It resembles a shorter and smaller-flowered *Inula magnifica*, and crossed the Atlantic with early settlers to become a feature of American colonial gardens. Interesting rather than beautiful, it is very much for gardeners who seek authenticity or court nostalgia.

DAHLIA 'BISHOP OF LLANDAFF'

A few years ago, when dahlias were cast into a sort of taste-warp, followers of garden fashion would fall over themselves to assert that they never, ever grew them. After a while, however, it became *de rigueur* to add, 'except for the 'Bishop of Llandaff', of course.' Dahlias have stormed back into fashion recently, but this nice, old cultivar is still the best – and most popular – of the bunch. So, why does it have the resilience to roll with the punches of horti-snobbery, and emerge unscathed at the other end? Simply, it is a very good plant. The 'Bishop of Llandaff', introduced in 1928, has a single or semi-double flower that marks it as being close to the species *Dahlia coccinea*. The Aztecs grew similar selections in their gardens, and so did the Victorians. The flowers are intensely scarlet with bright gold centres, but it is the foliage that gives the plant its distinction. Dahlia foliage is a great drawback, as it is usually plentiful, unattractive, and of a particularly deadly green. The 'Bishop', on the other hand, has attractively divided leaves of coppery-purple overlaid with a metallic sheen like the blueing patina on expensive shotgun barrels. The foliage alone would make it worth growing, but the furnace-red flowers put it into the league of 'must-have' garden plants.

The 'Bishop of Llandaff' sets good seed, and it is interesting to collect this and take pot-luck on the offspring. We had some marvellous forms this year, many shades of scarlet or crimson with dark foliage, but all diverse variations on a theme. Apart from this, treat this cultivar like any other dahlia, lifting the tubers in autumn, and storing them undercover over winter. Build up stocks by taking cuttings in spring – this is a dahlia you will want to grow in legions.

Inula magnifica

HELIANTHUS

I love giant herbaceous plants, and I also love anything that flowers late, prolonging at least the illusion of autumn bounty through October and even into November. So I regard the perennial sunflowers – the helianthus – with great affection, as they fulfil both criteria. These big bold daisies from North America are coarse of leaf, brassy of flower, but imposing and handsome. I have them with tall aconitums in a border pairing that does not even start to get underway until October, and they are also a mainstay of my autumn garden, where they grow with sky-blue *Salvia uliginosa*. They have been out of fashion in recent years, and I urge their rehabilitation.

Helianthus make robust clumps of typical sunflower foliage up to 2.2 m (7 ft) tall, topped off by the sort of simple yellow daisies a child might draw. They are marvellous for cutting, being just the ticket for the vast nostalgic flower arrangements that decorate country churches during the harvest festival, shedding earwigs on the chancel floor. Although I love them dearly, I have to concede that they do have faults. They are dreadful floppers unless firmly staked, and a collapsed clump can swamp many square yards of border. So stake early, stake strongly. *Helianthus atrorubens*, moreover, comes with a health warning: it is rampantly invasive. Choose a tamer variety, although none is exactly reticent. *Helianthus salicifolius* has narrow foliage, like a lily, and rather bright starry flowers. Of those I grow, *Helianthus quinquinervis* is big, floriferous, and a pleasant clear light yellow. *H.* 'Lemon Queen' is similar, and *Helianthus decapetalus* 'Capenoch Star' is shorter – a mere 1.2 m (4 ft) and semi-double. All are brilliant.

Finally, grow *Helianthus tuberosus* for your vegetable garden. Better known as Jerusalem artichoke, the tubers make one of the most delicious winter soups.

Dahlia 'Bishop of Llandaff'

DARK-EYE SUNFLOWER
Helianthus atrorubens

THE
BUTTERCUP
FAMILY

The varied and colourful blooms of the buttercup family can grace our gardens for four seasons of the year. There are blooms for the front and back of the border, annuals to use as infills and climbers to clothe our trees, as well as the odd tenacious weed.

RANUNCULACEAE

FLOWER FACTS
THE BIRDS AND THE BEES

THE FLOWERS FOUND in the buttercup family are so varied in appearance that you may wonder how on earth these plants are related; a closer look reveals a few shared family traits. The flowers are usually terminal, that is they are situated at the apex, or tip of the stem. To get to grips with the actual blooms it is helpful to know about flower structure (see page 8).

The members of the buttercup family have all used their sepals and tepals or petals in different ways to attract pollinators and, although they are classed as a primitive family, their flower designs are certainly spot-on.

The marsh marigold *(Caltha palustris)* and anemone have no petals at all. The brightly coloured flowers you see are made up of sepals. In clematis, the coloured parts of the flower are the tepals. The hellebores also have coloured sepals, which make up the showy part of the bloom, but look closely into the young flowers and you may spot the modified petals. These attractive tubular ruffles contain nectar and after pollination, when they are no longer required, they fall off. Fortunately for the gardener, the sepals remain for months to give one of the longest lasting flowers in the garden. The buttercup holds its nectar in pouches in the base of the petals, known as honey leaves, while aquilegias have well-developed nectaries, as well as coloured petals and sepals.

The aquilegias are stunning flowers, resembling a buttercup that has been morphed by a computer programme. Their sepals form a beautiful, often brightly coloured, five-pointed star which sets off the circle of often different coloured petals within. Although basically cup-shaped, the petals stretch out behind the sepals into long, drawn-out spurs, which hold a hidden treasure of nectar. Bizarre but beautiful. What insect could resist visiting them?

The fruits of the family are just as varied as the flowers. In love-in-a-mist *(Nigella damescana)*, balloon-shaped capsules covered in delicate tendrils swell up as the flower fades, and are every bit as decorative as the blooms. Buttercups have an attractive cluster of single-seeded fruits called achenes, and delphiniums produce long dry pods. Some members such as baneberries *(Actaea spicata,* for example*)* have fleshy fruits.

LEFT
COLUMBINE
Aquilegia

WILD BUTTERCUPS

MANY BUTTERCUPS and their relations are native to Britain and Europe. One familiar gardener's bane is the creeping buttercup *(Ranunculus repens)*. A common sight in damp soils, this common or garden weed reproduces by sending out runners and can spread as much as 3.5 sq m (11 sq ft) a year. Like its creeping cousin, the common meadow buttercup *(Ranunculus acris)*, also flowers from April to September; it is, however, more frequent in dry pastures along with the bulbous buttercup *(Ranunculus bulbosus)* which flowers from May to July. Shorter than *Ranunculus repens* and *Ranunculus acris*, its sepals, bent back over the stem, and its bulbous tubers are its distinguishing features. Less common is goldilocks *(Ranunculus auricomis)*, which is easily identified by its malformed or even absent petals. Another peculiarity is the mousetail *(Myosurus minimus)*, with its long, plantain-like head growing from the centre of its five to seven greenish-yellow petals.

Buttercups have many local names, including butterdaisy, eggs and butter and gold knobs, which are linked to the folklore that cows grazing the yellow fields produced more milk and butter. The bulbous buttercup was sometimes rubbed on cows' udders on May Day to increase milk yields. However, as they can inflame and blister the skin it is safer to stick to the child's folklore of holding a buttercup under your chin to see if you like butter. As for the cows, the hay was better than the pasture, as some buttercups are poisonous when fresh but not when dried.

LEFT
MARSH MARIGOLD
Caltha palustris

Lesser celandine (*Ranunculus ficaria*) is also regarded as a garden weed. It spreads rapidly in cultivated areas, splitting off its tiny corms when hoed to produce new plants. It does, however, have virtues. The beautiful flowers appear from March to May and really paint the spring yellow; their local Somerset and Dorset names, yellow stars and spring messengers, are very apt. Less appealing is the name pilewort, coined by the Doctrine of Signatures, by which plants were used to treat the ailment they resembled: celandine roots were thought to look like haemorrhoids. They were also used as a rat poison. Like the buttercup, this plant is poisonous, causing inflammation of the stomach which can be fatal. Crofters, who thought the tubers looked more like teats than piles, hung them in the byre in the hope that they would encourage milk production. Lesser celandine was thought to be Wordsworth's favourite plant. However, the plant engraved on his memorial in Grasmere looks more like the greater celandine, *Chelidonium majus*.

As many as 100 named forms of lesser celandine are now available, including the famous 'Brazen Hussy', with its chocolate leaves and golden flowers, the albus group, such as *R. ficaria* 'Randall's White', whose petals have slate-coloured backs, and the flore-pleno group, containing the double *R. f.* flore-pleno (syn. 'Knightshayes Double') which holds small, double flowers with green central eyes.

Other Ranunculaceae that have found a home both in and out of our gardens include the green and stinking hellebores, *Helleborus viridis* and *Helleborus foetidus*, and the columbine, *Aquilegia vulgaris*. The hellebores may be truly native to one or two of the southern counties of England, but are widely considered garden escapees. Traveller's joy *(Clematis vitalba)* is a wonderful, vanilla-scented climber which was named by the sixteenth-century herbalist John Gerard, who spotted it in nearly every hedgerow from Gravesend to Canterbury and so claimed it for travellers who would pass by. Its fluffy seed heads give it the name old man's beard.

The family derives its name from the Latin *rana*, a frog, because many of the genera like growing in damp places. Best known is the marsh marigold *(Caltha palustris)*. Its large polished yellow flowers earn it the name king cups. Other local names include verrucia, as it was used to cure warts, solsequia and sponsa solis, as it opens as the sun rises and closes as it sets. The common name marsh marigold dates from its use in church festivals in the Middle Ages: the flowers were devoted to the Virgin Mary. It was also used in May Day celebrations in garlands, and to decorate cottage thresholds.

RIGHT
TRAVELLER'S JOY
Clematis vitalba

THE FLOWERING YEAR

THE MAIN ATTRIBUTE of the buttercup family is year-round blooms. Hellebores start the year off and with a craftily placed cloche here or there can be coaxed into flower in January. The plants look good on high beds, where you can peer up into the flowers to see if seedlings have yielded spotted or shaded forms. For a splash of yellow among delicate creams and pinks, go for the winter aconite and the rare adonis, both small, both yellow, and both exquisite. As for climbers, the flowers of the unbeatable *Clematis cirrhosa* appear on the first frost free days bringing a drift of soft scent.

Spring heralds low-growing, delicate anemones such as *A. appenina*, *A. blanda* and *A. nemorosa* to brighten up path edges and shaded areas. Hellebores, having lost their tiny petals, still display their showy sepals. Low-growing pulsatillas appear in purple, blue and even dark red, their fluffy seed heads extending their all-too-short flowering season. Marsh marigolds colour the water's edges, followed by a spread of yellow onto land as buttercups, such as *Ranunculus gramineus* and the towering New Zealand *Ranunculus insignis*, appear. Clematis are in their element in spring, with *C. alpina*, *C. macropetala* and, for real flower power, *C. montana*.

JANUARY

EARLY FLOWERING CLEMATIS
Clematis cirrhosa (HWC)
January–March

FEBRUARY

SPRING ADONIS, YELLOW PHEASANT'S EYE
Adonis vernalis (HP)
February–March

SPRING ANEMONE
Anemone blanda (HP)
February–April

WINTER ACONITE
Eranthis hyemalis (HP)
February–March

HEPATICA
Hepatica nobilis (HP)
February–April

MARCH

FALSE RUE-ANEMONE
Isopyrum thalictroides (HP)
March–May

APRIL

RUE-ANEMONE
Anemonella thalictroides (HP)
April–June

CALLIANTHEMUM
Callianthemum coriandrifolium (HP)
April–June

MARSH MARIGOLD
Caltha palustris (HP)
April–May

ALPINE CLEMATIS
Clematis alpina (HWC)
April–May

PASQUE FLOWER
Pulsatilla vulgaris (HP)
April–May

NEW ZEALAND BUTTERCUP
Ranunculus insignis (HP)
April–June

MAY

JAPANESE COLUMBINE
Aquilegia flabellata (HP)
May–July

MEADOW RUE
Thalictrum aquilegiifolium (HP)
May–July

GLOBE FLOWER
Trollius europaeus (HP)
May–June

JUNE

RED BANEBERRY
Actaea rubra (HP)
June–July
(berries, July–October)

LARKSPUR
Consolida ambigua
(syn. *Delphinium consolida*) (HA)
June–August

LOVE-IN-A-MIST
Nigella damascena (HA)
June–August

BUTTERCUP
Ranunculus acris (HP)
June–August

JULY

MONKSHOOD
Aconitum napellus (HP)
July–August

BLACK SNAKEROOT
Cimicifuga ramosa (HP)
July–August

CLEMATIS
Clematis viticella (HWC)
July–September

DELPHINIUM
Delphinium grandiflorum (HP)
July

AUGUST

JAPANESE ANEMONE
Anemone hupehensis (HP)
August–October

ORANGE PEEL CLEMATIS
Clematis tibetana subsp. *vernayi*
'Orange Peel' (HWC)
August–October

DECEMBER

CHRISTMAS ROSE
Helleborus niger (HP)
December–March

In summer, delicate clematis give way to blousy, flowering hybrids. In the middle area of the border, buttercups are succeeded by trollius, cottagey columbines and cloudy drifts of thalictrum and nigella, soon backed by tall spires of blue delphiniums. Then comes monkshood, also best situated at the rear of a border.

In late summer, borders display creamy spires of cimicifugas overshadowing the insignificant actaea flowers, which come into their own in autumn with shiny red or white fruits. Anemones also return in autumn, the hupehensis species providing tall drifts of pink and white. Clematis are still in full bloom; delicate *C. viticella* and bright yellow *C. orientalis* gradually replace late hybrids. Herbaceous clematis look good in autumn borders, resembling campanulas rather than buttercups. And hidden among the perennials, a hellebore or two will extend its last blooms ready to embrace the hellebores of the new year.

KEY

A: annual B: biennial P: perennial S: shrub
WC: woody climber HH: half-hardy H: hardy

49

BUTTERCUP DIRECTORY

TYPE OF PLANT	(H) HEIGHT (S) SPREAD	CONDITIONS REQUIRED (SEE KEY)	PLANT TYPE AND CULTIVATION TIP	PROPAGATION
Aconitum napelleus	H 1.8 m (6 ft) S 1.8 m (6 ft)	◐☼◑✻✻✻	Herbaceous perennial. Slight shade enhances flower colour.	Division or fresh seed.
ANEMONE Anemone hupehensis 'Hadspen Abundance' A. x hybrida 'Whirlwind'	H 1.2 m (4 ft) S 1.2 m (4 ft)	◐☼◑✻✻✻	Herbaceous perennial. Requires staking.	Root cuttings when dormant. Use pencil-thick roots 2.5 cm (1 in long) in gritty compost.
Anemone trullifolia	H 15 cm (6 in) S 20 cm (8 in)	◐☼◑✻✻✻	Deciduous perennial. Add leaf mould to soil.	Propagate by seed or lift and divide clumps in spring.
Anemonella thalictroides (pink form, *A.t.* Schoaff's form, *A.t* 'Flora Plena').	H 20 cm (8 in) S 15 cm (6 in)	◐◑✻✻✻	Alpine perennial. Grows well in bulb frame.	Division.
Aquilegia flabellata, A. 'Sweet Lemon Drops', *A. viridiflora*	H 60 cm (2 ft) S 45 cm (18 in)	◐◐☼◑✻✻✻	Deciduous perennial. Keep moist to retain foliage all summer.	Seed and division.
Aquilegia 'Mellow Yellow'	H 60 cm (2 ft) S 45 cm (18 in)	◐◐☼◑✻✻✻	Deciduous perennial. As above.	Will come almost 100 per cent true from seed sown in spring or summer.
Caltha palustris	H 60 cm (2 ft) S 45 cm (18 in)	●☼✻✻✻	Deciduous perennial. Wet but well-drained soil.	Divide.
Cimicifuga racemosa 'Atropurpurea'	H 1.8 m (6 ft) S 90 cm (3 ft)	◐☼◑✻✻✻	Herbaceous perennial. Stake.	Fresh seed or division in spring.
CLEMATIS Clematis 'Fuji-musume'	H 3 m (10 ft) S 1.5 m (5 ft)	◐◐☼◑✻✻✻	Deciduous perennial. Prune hard in late winter.	Semi-hardwood cuttings in midsummer.
Clematis koreana	H 1.8–2.5 m (6–8 ft) S 1.5 m (5 ft)	◐◐☼◑✻✻✻	Deciduous perennial. Remove unwanted stems after flowering.	Semi-hardwood cuttings in midsummer. Sow seed as soon as it is ripe.
Clematis macropetala, C. alpina, C. montana	H 1.8–3 m (6–10 ft) S 1.5 m (5 ft)	◐◐☼◑✻✻✻	Deciduous perennial. As above.	Semi-ripe cuttings in early to midsummer.
Clematis 'Pink Fantasy'	H 1.5–1.8 m (5–6 ft) S 90 cm (3 ft)	◐◐☼◑✻✻✻	Deciduous perennial. Feed hybrids in spring or early summer.	Semi-hardwood cuttings in midsummer.

Name	Dimensions	Conditions	Description	Propagation
Clematis tibetana subsp. *vernayi* 'Orange Peel'	H 6 m (20 ft) S 1.8 m (6 ft)	◌◑☼◑✸✸✸	Deciduous perennial. Cut back hard in winter or early spring.	Semi-hardwood cuttings in midsummer. Sow seed as soon as ripe.
DELPHINIUM *Delphinium* 'Bruce'	H 1.8 m (6 ft) S 60 cm (2 ft)	◌◑☼✸✸	Deciduous perennial. Thin shoots in spring. Requires staking. Control slugs. Dead head after flowering	Pencil-thick basal cuttings in early spring. Divide roots in early spring.
Delphinium 'Fanfare'	H 2.2 m (7 ft) S 75 cm (30 in)	◌◑☼✸✸✸	Deciduous perennial. As above.	Division of roots is possible in early spring.
Delphinium 'Loch Leven'	H 1.5 m (5 ft) S 75 cm (30 in)	◌◑☼✸✸✸	Deciduous perennial. As above.	Division of roots is possible in early spring.
Delphinium 'Rosemary Brock'	H 1.5 m (5 ft) S 60 cm (2 ft)	◌◑☼✸✸✸	Deciduous perennial. As above.	Division of roots is possible in early spring.
Delphinium 'Sandpiper'	H 1.2 m (4 ft) S 60 cm (2 ft)	◌◑☼✸✸✸	Deciduous perennial. As above.	Division of roots is possible in early spring.
Delphinium grandiflorum	H 30 cm (1 ft) S 30 cm (1 ft)	◌☼✸✸✸	Alpine perennial.	Self-sown seedlings.
Helleborus orientalis	H 45 cm (18 in) S 45 cm (18 in)	◌☼✸✸✸	Perennial. Moisture retentive soil.	Seed and division.
Nigella damascena	H 60 cm (2 ft) S 30 cm (1 ft)	◌☼✸✸✸	Annual. Deadhead to prolong flowering.	Seed sown in spring.
PULSATILLA *Pulsatilla campanella. P. cernua, P. vulgaris*	H 15–20 cm (6–8 in) S 15–20 cm (6–8 in)	◌☼✸✸✸	Perennial. Resents transplanting.	Seed.
RANUNCULUS *Ranunculus insignis*	H 60 cm (2 ft) S 30 cm (1 ft)	◑●☼✸✸✸	Semi-evergreen perennial. Thrives in moist, well drained soil.	Propagate by seed or by dividing crowns of growth in spring.
Ranunculus lyallii	H 1.5 m (5 ft) S 45 cm (18 in)	◑●☼✸✸✸	Semi-evergreen perennial. Needs well-conditioned soil, cool environment.	Propagate by seed.
THALICTRUM *Thalictrum aquilegiifolium* var. *album*, *Thalictrum delavayi*	H 90 cm (3 ft) S 90 cm (3 ft)	◌◑☼◑✸✸✸	Herbaceous perennial. Woodland conditions.	Fresh seed or division.
Trollius europaeus	H 75 cm (2 ft 6in) S 90 cm (3 ft)	◑☼◑✸✸✸	Herbaceous perennial. Thrives in moist conditions.	Fresh seed or division.

KEY
◌ Well drained soil ◑ Moist soil ● Wet soil ☼ Sun ◑ Partial shade ✸ Tolerates full shade
✸ Half-hardy to 0°C (32°F) ✸✸ Frost-hardy to -5°C (23°F) ✸✸✸ Fully hardy to -15°C (5°F)

THE GARDENS
PLANT WORLD

Ray Brown's South Devon garden is the perfect place to study a wide range of plants in the buttercup family. Set on a north-east facing slope with magnificent views over Bishopsteignton and Lyme Bay, the beds of this two-acre garden are set out like a map of the world – ideal for a spot of instant globe-trotting.

I DID HAVE RESERVATIONS about a garden arranged like a map. Would it have a miniature Eiffel Tower rising from Europe and a model of the Statue of Liberty for North America? In fact, there are no gimmicks at Plant World, but there are plenty of unusual plants. Although the beds are not shaped very obviously like the countries they represent, they are in correct relationship to each other so the visitor does enjoy a sense of travelling from country to country. It is certainly fascinating to be aware of a plant's origins, and therefore its cultural needs.

Behind a fascinating garden there is usually an interesting character, and Ray Brown is best described as a romantic. Coventry born, he trained as a metallurgist, but on a whim, moved to Scotland to take up eel fishing. 'We ended up running a guest house in north-west Scotland, which soon developed into a nursery,' explained Ray, 'but we needed a warmer climate for plants.' Friends who gardened on Dartmoor helped Ray and his wife, Linda, come up with a concept for the garden, and the idea of Plant World was born.

LEFT
MOUNT COOK LILY, ROCKWOOD LILY, GIANT BUTTERCUP
Ranunculus lyalli

RIGHT
NEW ZEALAND BUTTERCUP
Ranunculus insignis

Although most Ranunculaceae originate from cooler northern regions of the world, there are some surprises from the southern hemisphere. The Mount Cook lily *(Ranunculus lyalii)* from New Zealand enjoys the accolade of being the largest buttercup in the world. It grows wild in semi-shaded positions created by rocks and taller plants, at altitudes of 450–1500 m (1500–5000 ft), where the air is constantly freshened by nearby waterfalls. In these ideal situations, it can reach 1.5 m (5 ft) in height, with thick, rounded leaves, 38 cm (15 in) across, and pure white flowers in spring and early summer.

Also from New Zealand and similar, but slightly smaller and yellow-flowered, is *Ranunculus insignis.* 'If you want to grow these giant buttercups well, they must never dry out,' explained Ray. 'Excavate their planting hole and add loads of well-rotted manure or compost, because their roots go down 30 cm (1 ft) or more.'

On my visit in late spring, we started in the Himalayan section of the gardens, where rain gently falling on poolside marsh marigolds *(Caltha palustris)* added to their natural charm. Although they grow wild in the Devonshire countryside, their wide distribution means they can also be found in the Himalayas, from Kashmir to Bhutan, at 122–1220 m (400–4000 ft). 'Marsh marigolds are easy to grow if you can give them moisture,' said Ray. 'They can be planted into borders, but will struggle unless the soil is damp.' Another Himalayan native, *Anemone trullifolia,* immediately caught our eye. 'Now this is the most desirable of all anemones,' enthused Ray. 'They can be white, or an indescribable, glistening blue. People have been known to fall in love with them, and I could sell thousands if I had them. Unfortunately, they don't set seed here, so I have to split clumps for more plants.'

ABOVE
Anemone trullifolia

RIGHT
Aquilegia
'Sweet Lemon Drops'

FAR RIGHT
Aquilegia 'Mellow
Yellow'

The small, delicate-looking flowers are white, but the petals have blue backs. There is a scarcer violet form.

In the European section of Plant World I was delighted to find one of my favourite buttercups, *Ranunculus gramineus*. The grass-like, blue-green leaves make a good foil to bright yellow flowers on clump-forming plants up to 50 cm (20 in) high. It is found in south-western regions of Europe in dry rocky hills. Perversely, in cultivation it prefers a richer soil and does quite well in a pot.

Lesser celandine *(Ranunculus ficaria)* is a familiar sight in Britain and other northern European countries. In fact, over-familiarity is its fault, as it can spread over borders and lawns as a weed. Ray grows the double flowered form, as both this and coloured-leaved forms like bronze *R. f.* 'Brazen Hussy' do not set seed and remain as neat clumps. 'They don't spread themselves around and cause problems,' said Ray, 'but after flowering, die back to underground tubers, leaving space for other plants. If we need more plants, the clumps can be divided.'

Anyone who grows the promiscuous aquilegia might have noticed yellow markings on some of the leaves of chance seedlings, but in Ray's nursery 'Mellow Yellow' is so reliable that the golden leaves come almost 100 per cent true from seed, and its white or milky-blue flowers can be used to lighten up shady places. Also impressive is *A.* 'Sweet Lemon Drops'. This robust plant has a solid dome of deliciously perfumed pendulous, lemon-yellow flowers. 'I find aquilegias easy to grow,' said Ray, 'but they need moisture to keep plenty of fresh foliage all summer. On drier soils, they tend to die back during the heat of summer and produce more foliage again in autumn.'

This tour around Ray's garden has persuaded me to take a more botanical approach to my own garden. By collecting together worldwide members of a plant family, fascinating comparisons can be made.

THE CLEMATIS GARDEN

To appreciate the beautiful blooms of clematis and explore their usefulness in a small garden, Anne Swithinbank made two visits to Mary Toomey in her Dublin garden. This proved a splendid opportunity to admire both early- and late-flowering types as well as discussing the tricky subject of pruning.

MARY'S SMALL BACK GARDEN, only 10 x 8 m (32 x 26 ft), is designed to be admired from a circular, sunken space in the middle, bounded by a low retaining wall and surrounded by inspired planting. Even without the clematis it would be a charming garden, well-furnished with a range of interesting shrubs. As well as providing a backbone of year-round interest, these shrubs play host to the clematis which grow through and up them, sometimes with as many as four clematis festooning one shrub.

From her early days as a child in Sri Lanka, Mary has been fascinated by plants. She came to Ireland to study natural sciences, and her desire for plant knowledge and a love of gardening grew in tandem. She lectured in biology and managed to combine motherhood with writing a number of biology text books for high schools. Brimful of enthusiasm for her subject, she edits the Clematis Society journal 'The Clematis' (see page 188), runs a gardening club, which she founded, and gives talks on a variety of horticultural topics, including clematis.

Standing in Mary's back garden, I was struck by the wonderful combination

LEFT
CHILEAN GLORY FLOWER
Eccremocarpus scaber
with *Clematis macropetala*

RIGHT
Clematis macropetala
'Albina Plena'
with *Clematis koreana*

LEFT
Clematis tibetana subsp.
vernayi 'Orange Peel'

RIGHT
Clematis 'Fuji-musume'

FAR RIGHT
Clematis 'Pink Fantasy'

of a semi-double, mauve-blue *C. macropetala* with the flame-coloured climber *Eccremocarpus scaber* (Chilean glory flower). Another support was shared by an intertwining of unusual, pure white, double-flowered *C. macropetala* 'Albina Plena' with dark, almost black maroon-purple *C. koreana* making a dramatic contrast.

Planting is very important. 'The best time is early autumn,' said Mary, 'and if you think of one guinea for the plant and two guineas for the hole, you won't go far wrong.' She uses well-rotted manure to enrich the planting hole. 'Larger-flowered hybrids should be planted deeper by some 10–12 cm (4–5 in) than in their pots,' she explained, 'this helps them survive clematis wilt if it strikes.' Plants often re-grow from below ground, even months after dying back. 'The species don't suffer from wilt. I always recommend *C. montana* and *C. viticella* for beginners, because they are easy to establish and grow.'

Clematis should not be planted too close to their host plant, or they will be starved of moisture. Planted to one side, they can be guided towards the host with canes until able to latch on with their leaf-stalk tendrils. Newly planted clematis should be pruned hard back in early spring to encourage shooting from the base.

Among the early-flowering clematis, *C. montana* is a great favourite with gardeners. Mary has trained the pale pink form, *C. montana* var. *rubens* over the pergola leading to her front garden. The inevitable bare stems at the base have been disguised by the evergreen shrub *Euonymus fortunei* 'Silver Queen'.

Mary has such an all-embracing love of plants that it seemed natural to ask what led her to specialize in clematis. 'A nature study lesson on seed dispersal at primary school started me off on the road to clematis growing, as I was fascinated by the seed heads of *Clematis vitalba* (old man's beard). Clematis are such accommodating plants for small gardens like mine.'

On my return visit in high summer, I really noticed how well the large-flowered mid- and late-season varieties had responded to their careful nursing. Garlanding trees and shrubs with their spectacular blooms, the body of each plant was full of fresh shoots and promising buds.

Mary drew my attention to C. 'Pink Fantasy'. 'This one is tolerant of wilt,' she explained, 'and you can see how the flowers change colour from rose-pink as they open, to a much paler pink with a slight stripe, then almost to white as they age.' Capitalizing on space, one stem is trained along the top of a low retaining wall and another into the gold-leaved evergreen shrub, *Escallonia laevis* 'Gold Brian'.

I could not believe that an impressive specimen of C. 'Fuji-musume', a relatively new Japanese variety, had been rescued from a rubbish pile at a nursery. Nursed back to health and grown in a large pot, it sported strong, deep-green leaves and massive shimmering blue flowers. In the back garden, the *Viburnum* x *bodnantense* 'Dawn' I remembered from spring had all but disappeared under a groaning mass of clematis foliage, seed heads and flowers. *C. tangutica* 'Helios' is a beauty with reflexed yellow tepals which fall leaving fluffy seed heads. It contrasts well with *Tropaeolum speciosum* (flame creeper). While *C. tangutica* 'Helios' remains compact, similar *C. tibetana* subsp. *vernayi* 'Orange Peel' is rampant and is more suited to a larger space. Both need to be pruned after flowering.

'Pruning can be complicated,' sympathized Mary. Double-flowered hybrids should not be pruned at all. The early-flowering types, which bloom before June, only need to be tidied up a little, immediately after flowering. Later-flowering types should be pruned in late winter or early spring. Cut them down to about 30 cm (1 ft), but not into old wood.

I left Mary to enjoy her garden. 'I like to think I have a William Robinson style,' she said, 'with great billowings of growth and plants looking at me from all corners.' Her parting shot, said with almost missionary zeal was: 'Clematis will do fine even without pruning. They are easy to grow, and everyone should try them.'

THE DELPHINIUM GARDEN

One of the stars of a classic herbaceous border is another showy member of the buttercup family, the delphinium. To admire top-quality blooms and understand the expertise needed to grow them, Anne Swithinbank joined Richard Wainwright in his garden near Leeds.

RICHARD'S BUNGALOW is built on a hill, and as we strolled down the lawn I admired the countryside view. 'I could never understand why the big house was not built up here,' said Richard. 'My father bought it in the 1930s with the 0.8 hectare (two acre) garden. After he died, we eventually sold the house and built our bungalow, keeping a large part of the original garden.'

The borders are hidden by a hedge, so the first view of them is on turning under an arch groaning with scented, pink rose Bantry Bay: the effect was breathtaking. 'The borders were designed so that when barren in winter, they would never spoil the view,' explained Richard. 'Even now, the hedge prevents us from staring at a middle ground of empty beds in winter.' In summer, they are full of delightful, yet not overpowering colour.

'I plant the delphiniums mainly in small groups of single colours,' he continued. They rise from among other plants that contrast with their blues, purples, pinks and whites; this way, each delphinium stands out as an individual. After flowering they die back ungracefully, but in these beds their old stems and browning leaves

LEFT
Delphinium 'Bruce'

RIGHT
**RICHARD
WAINWRIGHT'S
DELPHINIUM
BORDER**

are successfully disguised behind their border mates, which include red-flowered *Lychnis chalcedonica* (Maltese cross), varieties of astrantia (masterwort), phlox and achillea. There are also pillar roses such as 'Chinatown'.

Some delphiniums, like silvery purple 'Fanfare' are tall, with spikes rising 2.2 m (7 ft). Others, like 'Moonbeam', whose white flowers are greenish in the centre, add pale tones to the plantings. Dramatic violet-purples like 'Bruce' are welcome for their richness.

'My father started all this,' said Richard. 'Undaunted by the impermeable clay, he dug out the long double beds exactly as you see them today and thoroughly conditioned the soil.' Richard inherited the delphinium collection and has refined it by evaluating every plant, keeping the best and replacing the less worthy with better cultivars: he now has 66 different kinds. Dating from the original 1930s plantings are compact 'Lady Eleanor', a double-flowered blue with flashes of mauve, and sky-blue 'Mrs. Tommy Carlisle, a paler blue with shimmering lilac-mauve-centred flowers and lots of side-spikes. 'These older varieties tend to be daintier with subtle colours and more widely spaced flowers,' explained Richard.

Delphinium flowers deserve close scrutiny. They consist of five outer petal-like sepals and an 'eye' of eight inner petals, known as the 'bee'. The bee can vary in colour and often contrasts well with the sepals. 'Rosemary Brock' has 1.5 m (5 ft) tall spikes of dusky pink flowers which darken towards the edges of the sepals. The brown eye in the centre looks just like a furry bee. The dark centre of 'Sandpiper' makes the white of the sepals appear even purer.

Richard's plants, like most garden delphiniums, are of the Elatum Group and have many species in their parentage, mainly from the Himalayas and other mountainous regions.

RIGHT
Delphinium
'Sandpiper' and
D. 'Loch Leven'

BELOW LEFT
Delphinium
'Rosemary Brock'
and *D.* 'Sandpiper'

BELOW
Delphinium
'Fanfare'

'They are perfectly hardy,' said Richard, 'but they must have water. Imagine their natural habitat: the snows melting in spring, sending a steady trickling of water down to the roots. Their soil must not become stagnant and a windswept site will be a problem for all but dwarf, 90 cm (3 ft), varieties.' Although delphiniums need good light, they can suffer if exposed to too much scorching hot sun.

Work on established plants begins in March when the rash of new shoots has to be thinned down to three or four. 'When the shoots are 5–7.5 cm (2–3 in) above soil level, dig down and coax them from the parent plant with a small heel attached so they are 12.5–15 cm (5–6 in) long,' said Richard. 'This thinning is essential for good flower spikes, and I also believe it extends the life of an individual crown.' The shoots are used as cuttings: 'You can divide delphiniums, but our cuttings are so successful that we never do.'

Richard believes in feeding the soil rather than the plants, and every other year a top dressing of well-rotted manure is spread over the beds. Only the delphiniums that put out sideshoots to give a second flowering are treated to a summer liquid feed. Slug control is also essential, and must be in place virtually year-round.

Richard, a retired MP, now has trouble bending easily and is assisted by his gardener, Michael Graham. Michael previously worked for Leeds parks, who coincidentally hold the National Collection of delphiniums at Temple Newsam Park. The effort of growing these superb plants is rewarded by some six weeks of bloom, from late June to the end of July and even into August with some.

My only attempt at growing named delphinium varieties was doomed by hungry slugs, but newly inspired by this beautiful garden I will certainly try again.

PLANTSMAN'S CHOICE

BILL CHUDZIAK

HELLEBORES

Hellebores have become wildly fashionable in recent years. The Christmas and Lenten roses that once graced gardens in the dead of winter have been multiplied by breeding or selection into a multiplicity of cultivars, seed strains or forms. They are the collectors' plant *par exellence*. This is partly explained by the worthwhile trend towards year-round gardens, and anything that flowers so generously in our darkest days is to be cherished. But the chief reason for the allure of the hellebore is, quite simply, its beauty.

Everybody wants the Lenten rose, commonly known as *Helleborus orientalis* or *Helleborus* x *hybridus*. At the turn of the year the plants start to throw out their trusses of wonderful cupped flowers, each with a prominent central boss of starry stamens. Flowers come in a large range of strong colours, from glowing whites through creams and sulphur yellows, to fruity pinks and dark plums. Many are veined, freckled or stippled with chestnut-brown or claret; others are suffused with a contrasting pigment which either defines a central eye or stains the flower with translucent tints. 'Picotee' forms have the outer edge of the corolla delicately rimmed with a second colour. Best of all for lovers of dark flowers are the slatey blacks, sultry as quarried Welsh slate and wonderfully sophisticated: the floral equivalent of a dry Martini.

Helleborus niger, the Christmas rose, by contrast, has the colour and texture of candlewax. In the wild this plant varies widely, but the forms that are around in cultivation are mostly pale-flowered, set off by a boss of sumptuous yellow stamens. Look for one of the outstanding clones propagated by division, like 'Potter's Wheel', or a selected seed strain like the superlative 'Blackthorn Strain', washed with the palest porcelain pink.

Most gardens can provide the right conditions for these hellebores: a cool spot with soil that does not dry out, but is not waterlogged – wet feet means death. Dig a good hole and incorporate plenty of organic matter and a handful of limestone chippings if your soil is acid. And then be patient. Hellebores will flower more splendidly every year and in the depths of winter, when the rest of the garden seems dead, they enthral us with their annual affirmation of life.

ABOVE

HELLEBORE *Helleborus orientalis* hybrids

LEFT

JAPANESE ANEMONE *Anemone hupehensis* 'Hadspen Abundance'

ANEMONELLA THALICTROIDES

The botanical name of this little plant leaves us in no doubt as to which family it belongs; *Anemonella thalictroides* means 'the small anemone that resembles a thalictrum', and this strong family resemblance is a characteristic of the Ranunculaceae, where thalictrums look like aquilegias, and pulsatillas and anemones regularly exchange names.

Anemonella thalictroides is a native of the shady moist North American woodland that gives us some of our choicest spring plants. They seem to have in common a sort of crystalline beauty, and the unmistakable allure of plants with star quality.

RUE ANEMONE
Anemonella thalictroides (pink form)

PASQUE FLOWER
Pulsatilla vulgaris ssp. *anglicum*

LOVE-IN-A-MIST
Nigella damascena

This small plant enjoys the damp but well-drained leaf-soil of the forest floor. From a tuberous rootstock it produces a neat carpet of delicate trembling leaves and smooth flowering stems 20 cm (8 in) tall. These usually bear three starry flowers with white or pale pink petals, cupped and delicate like a wood anemone. The whole plant seems to have its cell system charged with moisture, and this is what gives it its pristine glistening appearance.

There have been various select and improved forms of this already first-rate plant. The pink form has shell-pink flowers, paling towards the centre. The central boss is a hard apple-green knot softened by a nimbus of cream stamens. More showy is the rare and desirable 'Schoaff's Double', which has layer upon layer of petals forming a crowded posy-like flower. It is of quite a strong pink, like Windolene®, intensifying towards the green button centre. All the anemonellas are hard to get hold of, although seed is often obtainable from specialist sources. 'Schoaff's Double' is desperately rare, so if you see it let me know, as I have been trying to acquire it for years.

PULSATILLA VULGARIS

It used to be said that Pasque flowers sprang up where the Danes shed their blood. It is a rare privilege to see pulsatillas growing exuberantly wild in the shallow chalky soil of a south-facing hillside, but we can all enjoy this exquisite plant as, like the hellebore, it is now much more common in gardens than in the wild.

In protected garden conditions, the pulsatilla performs quite differently. Wildlings hug the ground, dwarfed by exposure, competition, and the iron rations of a poor soil; garden plants are more expansive. Their plump buds emerge early out of the naked earth, and hummocks of soft, filigree foliage develop as the flowering stem elongates. The buds have no calyx but are protected by an overcoat of silky hairs and a feathery collar, the involucre.

Initially they have the softly swelling shape of an old-fashioned bottle, but open out into a perfect chalice, downy outside, rich violet within. Finally, the flower expands into a shallow six-petalled saucer, revealing a splendid central boss of golden stamens. The filmy involucre sits around the neck of the flower like an ostrich-feather boa. A short disreputable period follows as the flower fades, but resist the temptation to dead head as further glory is to come. The seed heads, like shocks of silky-fine baby hair, are beautiful for weeks.

Pulsatillas need sun, drainage and, ideally, a dash of lime. A raised bed is perfect as you can supply their needs and enjoy eye contact. Propagation is easy once you grasp that the seed must be fresh: take the seed tray to the plant. When the cool autumn rains come, seed germinates like cress. There have been some aberrations bred recently, doubles, fimbriated forms, unlikely colours. Leave them alone. Nothing beats the original. Except perhaps, if you can find it, the most desirable of all, the wonderful sky-blue 'Budapest Blue'.

NIGELLA DAMASCENA

Ephemeral hardy annuals have been overlooked in recent decades. Borders have been dominated by substantial perennials, or riotously colourful bedding plants, and old-fashioned annuals like love-in-a-mist have been relegated to children's gardens or are grown simply for cutting. But tastes change, and annuals are surging back into fashion.

BELOW
Delphinium grandiflorum

I encourage *Nigella damascena* to self-sow through my borders, and its slender and airy habit is just what is needed to fill gaps. This is a delicately beautiful plant with fine filigreed foliage. The best strain, 'Miss Jekyll', grows to 51 cm (20 in), and is topped by sky-blue, semi-double flowers. Comprised of two overlapping circlets of pointed blue sepals, five in each layer, they look like elegant Elizabethan ruffs. At their centre is a five-clawed cluster of carpels, and the whole is enveloped in a muzzy veil of foliage – the filmy involucre that gives the flower its charming nickname. Later, puffed-up seed capsules, horned like jesters' caps, are decorative until the first frosts, and dry well for the house. Still surrounded by a haze of involucre, they give the plant its alternative name of devil-in-a-bush. It is child's play to grow, but hates transplanting, so you must sow it where you want it. Thereafter, it self-sows, and has a happy knack of appearing where it looks best.

Delphinium grandiflorum is usually grown as an annual, although it flowers better in subsequent years. It makes a neat branching plant, sparse of foliage, but with unusually large flowers. In its best forms, it is an intense clear blue, lightly washed with mauve. The tilted buds really do look like shoals of dolphins, something first remarked upon by the ancient Greeks. It is rather a difficult plant to place; here at Craigieburn, it seeds around a raised bed among erodiums and celmisias, and when it flowers, everybody wants it.

TROLLIUS EUROPAEUS

To all appearances the globe flower is a buttercup: it has the same foliage, the same tough hollow stems, the same cupped yellow flowers. But it is the buttercup made sublime. Garden writer Deborah Kellaway calls it 'the apotheosis of the common buttercup, its ascent into heaven'. It flowers, in southern Scotland, on the cusp of spring and summer, so it coincides with that wonderful season when everything is ripe with promise. The flowers are generous incurving globes, consisting of up to ten overlapping sepals enclosing the same number of thin petals. The petals are scarcely bigger than stamens, so it is the arrangement of sepals which we call the flower. The texture is wonderful, substantial, waxy, but at the same time translucent, and the colour is a refined pale lemon completely without stridency. Visitors to our garden have occasionally mistaken it for that undisputed border aristocrat *Paeonia mlokosewitschii*. It likes a damp position, so is a good pondside plant, although equally at home in a well-cultivated border, where, with *Dicentra spectabilis*, it usually kicks off the herbaceous season.

Most other members of the genera are asiatics. *Trollius chinensis* (syn. *T. ledebourii*) has orange-yellow sepals surrounding a cluster of upward-pointing spiky petals. It has been crossed with *Trollius europaeus* to produce some worthwhile offspring. 'Feuertroll' is orangey yellow, as is 'Orange Princess', while the highly desirable 'Alabaster' is ivory. All resemble their European parent in form. But, for once, the European species takes its crown from the asiatic, so if you only grow one, make sure it is our own.

ACONITUM

It is the last week of October, and my border is dominated by a 2.2 m (7 ft) tall clump of *Aconitum carmichaelii,* fresh and untroubled by the wind and driving rain of autumn. The form I grow is a singing azure-blue, touched and veined with violet, but others are the inky blue, more usually associated with the genus. At first glance, the individual flowers seem to look blindly at the world, visored by the hooded sepal at their apex. They appear helmeted like Darth Vader, with a sinister and unsettling beauty. Look more closely, though, and you will see that beneath each hood is a cupped flower, centred with a spherical cluster of stamens. It looks entirely typical of the Ranunculaceae.

At the other end of the year I love the delicacy of new aconitum foliage. Neat and filigreed, it has a slight bronze sheen that looks brilliant with tulips and young garnet-red peony leaves.

In midsummer, *Aconitum napellus* ssp. *vulgare* 'Carneum' is an eye-catcher, with narrow spires of soft pinky flowers, over much-divided, holly-green foliage. 'Bressingham Spire' is a more typical napellus, navy-blue and somewhat later flowering. The earliest aconitum, the ivory-cream 'Ivorine', a hybrid of unknown parentage, grows happily in woodland with primulas and foxgloves.

Best of all, though, is the annual fanfare from the sensational *Aconitum* x *cammarum* 'Bicolor'. In Scotland, the narrow crowded spires of flowers, white heavily margined with blue, easily reach 1.8 m (6 ft). Each colour appears to bleed into the other, rather like the fugitive dyes on ethnic cottonstuffs. Fantastic.

Keep aconitum away from children, as the plant has been used as a poison from time immemorial. Perhaps our awareness of this dark and secret side enhances the sinister allure of this genus, a feeling perfectly understood by the marvellous garden writer, Deborah Kellaway. Of aconitum as garden plants, she writes: 'They supply the shadow that accompanies the light.'

THALICTRUM AQUILEGIIFOLIUM

The thalictrums are sterling performers for the mid- to late summer garden, and *Thalictrum aquilegiifolium* starts the season in June. It is an elegant plant, delicate and airy, but there is nothing effete or wishy-washy about it and, despite its apparent fragility, it is both stately and majestic. The foliage appears first, superficially resembling that of its cousin the aquilegia, but it is more beautiful in form and colour. Branching and pinnate, it is presented on stems as thin as jewellers' wire, the cool blue-green leaflets are strongly reminiscent of a maidenhair fern. The flowering stems, mahogany overlaid with a sloe-like bloom, branch upwards to about 90 cm (3 ft) terminating in panicles of dozens of tiny

RIGHT

GLOBE FLOWER *Trollius europaeus*

spherical buds, pale lilac in colour. The sepals that hold these buds drop away, and the flowers explode into balls of creamy-white fuzz, each a tiny pyrotechnic incident. Closer examination reveals them to be devoid of petals and composed entirely of stamens. Clusters of filaments make up the foamy flowers, each tipped by a trembling pollen-bearing anther. A flowering panicle is like a billow of cumulus cloud, and although its individual elements are thin and fragile, the whole plant has a strong presence in a border. The type plant is a little taller, with puffs of rosy lilac flowers that combine wonderfully with crimson and claret roses.

Thalictrums are easy to grow, preferring good moist soil and cool conditions. They always seem to be at their most delectable in the cooler damper climate of the west, but in drier areas they thrive in the microclimate of a poolside planting, or in shade. Try to place the plant where it can be seen, as it were, from the knees up, allowing it to display to the full its amazing style, grace, and lightness of touch.

CIMICIFUGA

The best place to grow cimicifuga is in woodland. In late September, just when understorey vegetation has assumed a faint aura of decay, they send up their cream exclamation marks of flower, all the more spectacular against a background of shadow. A century ago they were considered a coarse plant suitable only for rough areas, but tastes change, and we regard them as choice beauties, high in the desirability stakes.

Cimicifuga racemosa, or black snake root, has thin tensil stems, which rocket to 1.8 m (6 ft) or more, and elegant divided leaves strongly resembling those of its actaea cousins. The dark stems rise above the mounds of foliage and divide into a complex system of branches, each a narrow flower spire. Buds, open flowers and spent flowers perform separately but simultaneously, and herein lies peculiar decorative appeal. Tight spherical buds clothe the stems like rows of beads, each distinct from its neighbour. Opening flowers explode into fluffy balls of stamens, melding together to make fuzzy bottle-brush inflorescences. Fading flowers retain their form, but dwindle in substance, and as the wildly branching stems do not grow strictly upright, but weave and veer from the vertical, the effect is of shooting fireworks trailing meteor-tails of creamy stamens.

Cimicifuga ramosa comes from the eastern USA, but the majority of the genus originates from Japan and Korea.

LEFT

MONKSHOOD *Aconitum* 'Bressingham Spire'

70

Cimicifuga simplex is a shorter oriental species, only 90 cm (3 ft) high. 'Elstead' and 'White Pearl' are readily available cultivars, the former having purplish stems and pink tinged buds, whereas the latter has green stems and buds.

The most desirable – and expensive – cultivar is *Cimicifuga ramosa* 'Atropurpurea', and its variant 'Brunette', in which the entire plant is suffused with a smoky purple pigment save for the flowers, which are pinky white. It is lovely, but so is each and every one of them.

JAPANESE ANEMONES

The wonderful garden plants which we know as Japanese anemones are not from Japan at all, although they have probably been naturalized there for centuries. Most of the plants we grow are named cultivars, deriving from three Chinese and Himalayan species, *Anemone hupehensis*, *Anemone tomentosa* and *Anemone vitifolia*. The exact parentage of these hybrids is often murky and invariably confusing, but fortunately we can categorize the majority of them under the umbrella term of *Anemone* x *hybrida,* and let the botanists argue about the rest.

Their season is from late summer onwards, when the borders are dominated by jolly daisy-flowers in various shades of yellow or mauve; and the anemones' cool poise and crisp cupped flowers are a satisfying counterpoint to all the tousled exuberance of autumn.

Their leaves are roughly vine-shaped, their buds small tight spheres nodding gracefully on wiry stems: a wonderful foil for the first flowers. These are mostly six-petalled shallow cups of pink or white. At the centre, inside a circlet of pollen-laden golden stamens, is a hard green knot, comprising the female reproductive parts, packed tight.

As to colour, the pinks predominate over the whites. 'Prinz Heinrich', a deep rose-pink, is semi-double, while 'Königin Charlotte' and 'September Charm' are paler pink singles. Particularly beautiful is the deep pink 'Hadspen Abundance', bred by the great hybridist Eric Smith.

All the whites are wonderful. 'Honorine Jobert' seems to be readily available, and is a rangy and stylish five-footer. 'Whirlwind' is a white semi-double, bred in America, and 'Luise Uhink' has generously large semi-double flowers.

Japanese anemones tolerate sun or semi-shade, but prefer cool retentive soil. They often sulk for a year or so after planting but, once established, can colonize large areas and actually become quite thuggish. The solution to this is to place them where they can have their head. These plants are simply too good to curb.

MEADOW RUE
Thalictrum aquilegiifolium var. *album*

BUGBANE
Cimicifuga ramosa

JAPANESE ANEMONE
Anemone x *hybrida* 'Whirlwind'

THE
MINT
FAMILY

There are more in the Labiatae family than mints, and these plants do far more than flavour your food. The family includes some stunning herbaceous flowers and shrubs, ranging from the purple lavenders, which look fantastic en masse, to the fine, individual blooms of the salvias.

LABIATAE

FLOWER FACTS
THE BIRDS AND THE BEES

MOST LABIATES are herbaceous or shrubby, and many come from the Mediterranean; a few relations inhabit remote regions from the Arctic to the Himalayas. Quite an easy family to identify, they have several distinguishing features. Firstly, their regimental characteristics. The stems tend to be square and the leaves simple and sometimes hairy, with each pair arranged at right angles to the next. Next, their aroma. One of the most remarkable things about the smelly labiates is that, in general, the flowers are not scented. It is the epidermal glands on the leaves which emit the fragrant oils with that wonderful aromatic scent reminiscent of hot Mediterranean summer holidays.

Most of these oils do far more than just smell good. They may serve to keep away browsing animals, or to protect the plant from the heat of the Mediterranean sun. One oil, a terpene, exuded from the leaves of chaparral sage (*Salvia leucophylla*), acts as a growth inhibitor on neighbouring grasses. Clever stuff! People have also exploited these essential oils, and the family is renowned for its culinary and medicinal values. Thyme, rosemary and mint, all labiates, are used as a flavouring in many of our meals. Sage has been used for centuries as a culinary herb as well as a preservative agent. Pogostemon is the source of patchouli oil, and lavenders oils are used in aromatherapy to relieve stress.

As well as having oily attributes, this family could also win prizes for flower design. The blooms tend to be funnel- or bell-shaped with five fused sepals and five fused petals, usually containing both male and female parts. The flowers are often small but exquisitely formed with their lower, lipped petals designed as a landing stage for insects. In many flowers the nectar is hidden deep in the throat behind hairs or folds in the petals, so the visiting insects have to do their job and pollinate the flower before they get a reward. In the salvias, the stamens, which carry the pollen, have an articulated joint. When the pollinator, such as an insect or hummingbird, arrives, it thrusts its head deep into the flower and knocks into the back of the stamen. This brings down the other end, the anther, on to the pollinator's head or back, showering it with pollen. As the family has fragrant leaves, the flowers have to find a different way of attracting the insects. Australian mint bush (*Prostanthera*), a very aromatic labiate, has small white flowers with purple spots running into the centre of the bloom. These 'bee lines' act like runway lights directing the insect right to their goal: the nectar.

After pollination, results are small; you do not get many seeds out of one flower. Typically, the fruit from a single flower contains four one-seeded achene-like nutlets. Yet some of the best things come in small packages, and seeds from plants such as *Salvia patens* 'Cambridge Blue' are certainly worth saving and growing on.

LEFT
Salvia patens

WILD MINTS

MEMBERS OF THE MINT family are found in many parts of Europe, and several genera grow wild in Britain. Their flowers may be small, but their powerful properties more than make up for it. Corn mint, (*Mentha arvensis*), found in hedgerows and cornfields, has a true minty smell. It was once placed in cheeses to prevent them going off and rubbed inside bee hives to prevent the bees straying. The round-leaved mint, (*Mentha suaveolens*), smells of apples, while the pennyroyal (*Mentha pulegium*) has a peppermint scent. Pennyroyal, found throughout southern Europe, England and Wales, is often used in tea as a cold remedy. Its name, however, comes from '*pulex*', a flea, as it is a flea repellant. It was even used by royalty, hence the name pennyroyal! The mint that is found in marshes and in fens is a different species: *Mentha aquatica*. One variety, *M. a.* 'Crispa', with curled leaves, is a source of spearmint.

Wild thyme (*Thymus serpyllum*) with its tiny heads of pink flowers, is the creeping thyme of herb gardens. Garden cultivars have varying appearances; *T.s. coccineus* has bright red flowers and *T. s.* 'Goldstream' has variegated leaves. Common thyme (*Thymus vulgaris*), the usual culinary variety, comes from the Mediterranean, as does sweet marjoram *(Origanum majorana)* which, along with common marjoram (*Origanum vulgare*), a British species, is used as a culinary herb.

Catmint (*Nepeta cataria*) grows wild throughout Europe and is often found in the herb garden. Cats adore smelling it and sitting on it, but if the foliage is not

LEFT
BETONY
Stachys officinalis

wilted or bruised they (theoretically) leave it alone. The leaves can be made into a tea, said to calm a fever, and legend relates that chewing the root gives courage, a remedy used by a certain hangman before public performances!

Salvias are well known as both herbs and ornamentals. The native clary sage (*Salvia verbenaca*), is found throughout Europe. It has a pretty spike of purplish-blue flowers, but it was the seeds that were once sought after. The mucilage that forms on the moistened seeds was placed under the eyelids and, with the help of tears, helped wash dirt from the eye; hence its other name, Christ's eye.

Betony (*Stachys officinalis*) grows in woods and copses. With its spike of purple flowers, it also makes an attractive addition to the border, and in the open in good soil grows into a much showier plant. It was widely grown in physic gardens and was reputed to cure 47 diseases and ailments, including headaches, neuralgia, jaundice, gout and rheumatism. The leaves were also used as a snuff and as a yellow dye. Gypsywort (*Lycopus europaeus*), with elegant toothed leaves, was also used as a dye. A black liquid obtained from the leaves was used to colour wool and silk, and gypsies were said to use it to stain their skins darker.

Self heal (*Prunella vulgaris*) and bugle (*Ajuga reptans*) are both wound herbs, used externally as a poultice and internally as an infusion. Native throughout Europe, self heal has also become naturalized in North America where it is called blue curls due to its dense head of flowers. Ajuga cultivars have become popular in the garden for their colourful foliage and spikes of pink and purple flowers. For a good blue flower spike and large leaves, try 'Catlin's Giant', which does well in dry shade.

Some labiates, such as the dead nettles, are regarded as garden weeds rather than herbs. The white dead nettle (*Lamium album*) is often avoided by ardent weeders as it resembles, but is totally unrelated to, the stinging nettle. This is a real country child's plant: some, after picking off the flowers, taunted their friends with the plants pretending they were nettles; other (less sadistic) youngsters used to make whistles out of sections of the hollow stems. The plant is nicknamed 'Adam and Eve' as the stamens lying inside the flower look like two people side by side in bed.

One of the prettiest wild members is *Lamium galeobdolon,* the aptly named yellow archangel. The serrated leaves show off the beautiful whorls of hooded yellow flowers, which have red spots on their lower lips to guide the bees to the nectar. Its name comes from the Greek '*gale*', a weasel, whose face the flowers are said to resemble, and '*bdolos*', a bad smell – named not after the flowers, but the leaves. An infusion of the flowers is said to enliven the spirits and make the heart merry – a fitting remedy from a bright little plant.

RIGHT
CATMINT
Nepeta mussinii

WILD MINTS

BUGLE
Ajuga reptans

COMMON HEMP NETTLE
Galeopsis tetrahit

GROUND IVY
Glechoma hederacea

YELLOW ARCHANGEL
Lamium galeobdolon syn.
Galeobdolon luteum

WHITE DEAD NETTLE
Lamium album

RED DEAD NETTLE
Lamium purpureum

MOTHERWORT
Leonurus cardiaca

GYPSYWORT
Lycopus europaeus

WATER MINT
Mentha aquatica

CORN MINT
Mentha arvensis

PENNYROYAL
Mentha pulegium

CATMINT
Nepeta cataria

MARJORAM
Origanum vulgare

SELF HEAL
Prunella vulgaris

CLARY SAGE
Salvia verbenaca

LESSER SKULLCAP
Scutellaria minor

BETONY
Stachys officinalis

HEDGE WOUNDWORT
Stachys sylvatica

WOOD SAGE
Teucrium scorodonia

WILD THYME
Thymus serpyllum

COMMON THYME
Thymus vulgaris

THE FLOWERING YEAR

THE MINT FAMILY can provide garden blooms from March to November: with about 200 genera and 3000 species, there is certainly plenty of scope.

The season opens with one of the best-known members, rosemary (*Rosmarinus officinalis*), flowering from March until September. The species has pale blue-mauve flowers but varieties include *R. o.* var. *albiflorus* with white flowers. 'Roseus' and 'Majorca Pink' with pink flowers and 'Benenden Blue' and 'Fota Blue' with dark blue flowers.

Glechoma hederacea also produces lilac-blue flowers from March to June. An attractive variegated form is often used for flower and foliage effect in hanging baskets. The native dead nettles, both white and red, have a very long flowering season, from March to November. Their garden relative, *Lamium garganicum*, has beautiful pink flowers from late May to July and makes excellent groundcover. If cut back after flowering it retains its neat habit, and many produce a second flush at the end of the summer.

Prostantheras, the mint bushes from Australasia, have fragrant foliage and very attractive blooms. Spring-flowering species include *P. cuneata,* with white blooms flushed with lilac, and *P. ovalifolia*, supporting masses of soft lilac-mauve or purple flowers. The season is extended by the summer-flowering species. All in all, this is a group of shrubs that really deserves to be more widely grown.

Lavenders take us into the summer with *L. stoechas* and *L. angustifolia*, and on into early autumn with *L. multifida*, *L. lanata* and *L. dentata*. In June and July, they are joined by a multitude of pinks, blues and mauves as the herb garden burgeons with flowers such as betony, calamint, bergamot bee balm, catmint, marjoram, self heal and skullcap.

MARCH

GROUND IVY
Glechoma hederacea (HP)
March–June

ROSEMARY
Rosmarinus officinalis (H/HHS)
March–September

MAY

GIANT DEAD NETTLE
Lamium orvala (HP)
May–July

FRENCH LAVENDER
Lavandula stoechas (HSP)
May–July

MINT BUSH
Prostanthera cuneata (H/HHS)
May

JUNE

ACINOS
Acinos corsicus (HP)
June–September

MEXICAN GIANT HYSSOP
Agastache mexicana (HHP)
June–September

BUGLE
Ajuga reptans (HP)
June–July

BALLOTA
Ballota pseudodictamnus (HP)
June–September

BALM OF GILEAD
Cedronella canariensis (HP)
June–September

LAMIUM
Lamium garganicum (HP)
June–July

LEMON BALM
Melissa officinalis (HP)
June–July

BELLS OF IRELAND
Moluccella laevis (HHA)
June–September

BERGAMOT BEE BALM
Monarda didyma (HP)
June–September

CATMINT
Nepeta cataria (HP)
June–September

MARJORAM
Origanum vulgare (HP)
June–September

PHLOMIS
Phlomis longifolia (HPS)
June–July

JERUSALEM SAGE
Phlomis fruticosa (HSP)
June–July

SELF HEAL
Prunella vulgaris (HP)
June–November

JUNE

PINEAPPLE SAGE
Salvia elegans (HHSP)
June–September

CLARY
Salvia viridis syn.
S. horminum (HHA)
June–September

WINTER SAVORY
Satureja montana (HP)
June–October

SKULLCAP
Scutellaria galericulata (HP)
June–September

SCUTELLARIA
Scutellaria rivularis (HP)
June–July

BETONY
Stachys officinalis (HP)
(syn. *Betonica officinalis*)
June–October

WALL GERMANDER
Teucrium x *lucidrys* (HP)
June–August

WILD THYME
Thymus serpyllum (HP)
June–September

JULY

COMMON CALAMINT
Calamintha sylvatica (HP)
July–September

HYSSOP
Hyssopus officinalis (HP)
July–September

PENNYROYAL
Mentha pulegium (HP)
July–October

OBEDIENT PLANT
Physostegia virginiana (HP)
July–September

BLUE SAGE
Salvia patens (HHP)
July–September

AUGUST

BASIL
Ocimum basilicum spp. (HHA)
August

RUSSIAN SAGE
Perovskia atriplicifolia (HSP)
August–September

PERENNIAL SALVIA
Salvia guaranitica (HH sub-S)
August–October

SEPTEMBER

LION'S EARS
Leonotis leonurus syn.
L. ocymifolia (HHSP)
September–November

Thyme produces a mass of low-growing flowers for the front of the herb garden or border, and can be used in cracks in paths to give a flowering summer carpet. At the back of the border or in the shrubbery, phlomis bring in a bit of height and colour variation with the well known Jerusalem sage (*P. fruticosa*) and other yellow shrubby species, as well as the desirable pink *P. italica*. As the flowers fade, the shrubby perovskias take over, their grey foliage a perfect foil to their blue flowers. As with most labiates, they need a sunny, well-drained spot. In the mid front of the herbaceous and herb borders, hyssop and pennyroyal join the many summer herbs which carry on into August and September, to merge with the pink spires of the physostegias.

The stars of the family and of the late summer and autumn border are, however, the salvias. The annual *Salvia horminum* (syn. *S. viridis*) with its coloured bracts, and varieties of dwarf bedding salvias brightly decorate annual borders. Herbaceous borders sport the velvety blue spires of *S. patens* and the fantastic range of shrubby salvias starting with varieties of *S. microphylla* and *S. greggii* in reds and pinks, going on to the later, tall blue *S. guaranitica* and tall ice-cream-pink *S. involucrata*, both of which flower until the frosts. All are slightly tender and grow best in a sheltered south-facing spot with light soil, or alternatively in a cool greenhouse. Finally, a burnt-orange flower to go with the autumnal hues: *Leonotis leonurus*. A very unusual colour for a labiate, and well worth trying as a conservatory plant.

KEY
A: annual B: biennial P: perennial S: shrub
HH: half-hardy H: hardy

MINT DIRECTORY

TYPE OF PLANT	(H) HEIGHT (S) SPREAD	CONDITIONS REQUIRED (SEE KEY)	PLANT TYPE AND CULTIVATION TIP	PROPAGATION
Ballota pseudodictamnus	**H** 60 cm (2 ft) **S** 90 cm (3 ft)	◌☼❋❋❋	*Evergreen perennial. Likes dry conditions.*	*Cuttings and seed.*
Hyssopus officinalis	**H** 60 cm (2 ft) **S** 75 cm (30 in)	◌☼❋❋❋	*Deciduous perennial. Feed and water well in summer for growth.*	*Sow seed in autumn. Take softwood cuttings in summer.*
Lamium orvala	**H** 60 cm (2 ft) **S** 1.2 m (4 ft)	◌●❋❋❋	*Perennial. Less invasive than other lamiums.*	*Cuttings and seed.*
LAVANDULA *Lavandula angustifolia* 'Twickel Purple'	**H** 60 cm (2 ft) **S** 90 cm (3 ft)	◌☼❋❋❋	*Evergreen perennial. Trim flower heads after fading. Shorten further in spring for compact growth.*	*Semi-hardwood cuttings in summer.*
Lavandula stoechas 'Marshwood'	**H** 60 cm (2 ft) **S** 45 cm (18 in)	◌☼❋❋	*Evergreen perennial. Grow in a pot and move under cover during cold, damp weather.*	*Semi-hardwood cuttings in summer.*
Leonotis leonurus (syn. *Leonotis ocymifolia*)	**H** 1.8 m (6 ft) **S** 90 cm (3 ft)	◌☼❋	*Tender semi-evergreen perennial. Excellent conservatory shrub.*	*Cuttings and seed.*
Moluccella laevis	**H** 60–90 cm (2–3 ft) **S** 60 cm (2 ft)	◌☼❋❋	*Annual. Enjoys a fertile, very well drained, sunny spot.*	*Seed in spring.*
Monarda 'Squaw'	**H** 90 cm (3 ft) **S** 60 cm (2 ft)	◌◑☼◐❋❋❋	*Deciduous perennial. Water during droughts.*	*Lift, divide and replant in spring. Basal cuttings in spring.*
PHLOMIS *Phlomis longifolia*	**H** 1.8 m (6 ft) **S** 1.8 m (6 ft)	◌☼❋	*Evergreen shrub. Trim damaged growth in spring.*	*Cuttings and seed.*
P. italica, P. bovei ssp. *bovei*	**H** 1.2 m (4 ft) **S** 1.8 m (6 ft)	◌☼❋❋	*Evergreen shrub.*	*Cuttings and seed.*
Physostegia angustifolia	**H** 90 cm (3 ft) **S** 90 cm (3 ft)	◌☼❋❋❋	*Herbaceous perennial. Likes fertile soil.*	*Division in spring.*

Prostanthera cuneata 'Fastigiata'	**H** 90 cm (3 ft) **S** 45 cm (18 in)	◐☼◐❋❋	*Evergreen shrub.* *Must have well-drained* *soil to survive low* *temperatures.*	*Semi-ripe cuttings* *in late summer.*
SALVIA *Salvia elegans*	**H** 1.8 m (6 ft) **S** 90 cm (3 ft)	○☼❋❋	*Evergreen perennial.* *Needs winter minimum* *of 30°C (86°F).*	*Shoot-tip cuttings in* *spring and summer.*
Salvia involucrata 'Bethellii'	**H** 1.5 m (5 ft) **S** 90 cm (3 ft)	○☼❋	*Semi-evergreen* *perennial.* *Needs plenty of water* *in summer.*	*Shoot-tip cuttings* *in spring and summer.*
Salvia officinalis	**H** 75 cm (30 in) **S** 75 cm (30 in)	○☼❋❋❋	*Evergreen perennial.* *Prune hard in spring.*	*Semi-hardwood* *cuttings during* *summer.*
Salvia patens 'Cambridge Blue'	**H** 45–60cm (18–24in) **S** 45 cm (18 in)	○☼❋❋	*Half-hardy perennial.* *Store tuber over winter.*	*Shoot-tip cuttings in* *spring or summer.*
Salvia sclarea	**H** 90 cm (3 ft) **S** 60 cm (2 ft)	○◐●☼❋❋❋	*Evergreen biennial.* *Can transplant rosette* *in autumn.*	*Sow in early summer.*
Annual Salvias *Salvia horminum* (syn. *S. viridis*), *S. fulgens*	**H** 30 cm (1 ft) **S** 30 cm (1 ft)	○☼❋❋	*Annual.* *Fertile, well-drained soil.*	*Seed in spring.*
Salvia x jamensis 'James Compton'	**H** 90 cm (3 ft) **S** 75 cm (30 in)	○☼❋❋	*Evergreen perennial.* *Prune in spring.*	*Soft cuttings in spring.* *Semi-ripe cuttings in* *summer.*
Salvia x jamensis 'La Luna'	**H** 90 cm (3 ft) **S** 75 cm (30 in)	○☼❋❋	*Evergreen perennial.* *As above.*	*Soft cuttings in spring.* *Semi-ripe cuttings in* *summer.*
Salvia guaranitica	**H** 1.5 m (5 ft) **S** 60 cm (2 ft)	○☼❋❋	*Sub-shrub.* *Good on light soils.*	*Shoot-tip cuttings* *in spring and summer.*
Salvia microphylla	**H** 90 cm (3 ft) **H** 1.2 m (4 ft)	○☼❋❋	*Evergreen sub-shrub.* *As above.*	*Soft cuttings in spring.* *Semi-ripe cuttings in* *summer.*
Stachys coccinea	**H** 60 cm (2 ft) **S** 60 cm (2 ft)	○☼❋	*Tender perennial.* *Protect over winter.*	*Cuttings and seed.*
Teucrium x lucidrys	**H** 30 cm (1 ft) **S** 30 cm (1 ft)	○☼❋❋❋	*Perennial.* *Good edging plant.*	*Cuttings.*
Thymus pulegioides	**H** 5–25 cm (2–10 in) **S** 30 cm (1 ft)	○☼❋❋❋	*Evergreen perennial.* *Trim back after* *flowering, but not into* *old wood.*	*Seed in spring.* *Divide and replant in* *spring. Semi-ripe* *cuttings in summer.*

KEY

○ Well drained soil ◐ Moist soil ● Wet soil ☼ Sun ◐ Partial shade ❋ Tolerates full shade
❋ Half-hardy to 0°C (32°F) ❋❋ Frost-hardy to -5°C (23°F) ❋❋❋ Fully hardy to -15°C (5°F)

THE GARDENS
JEKKA'S HERB FARM

Many herbs are members of the Labiatae family. Summer gardens are enriched by their perfumes and colours; shut your eyes and you can almost hear the droning of bees over lavender and thyme. Anne Swithinbank visited Jekka McVicar, a personality on the horticultural show circuit, to see her herb farm near Bristol.

JEKKA HAS BEEN MANY things in her life, including playing a hippy flautist in Doctor Who and a musician in a 1970s pop band. Although her interest in herbs spans the last 20 years, it was only in 1985 that she really began to indulge this passion by setting up her own nursery. Initially, she and her family lived in a mobile home on the 1 hectare (2.5 acre) site. Potting sheds, standing grounds and polythene tunnels for the herbs were more important than upgrading the existing cottage, which the family moved into more recently. Its mellow walls make an ideal backdrop to the lavenders growing in the narrow front garden.

Given plenty of sun and well-drained soil, lavenders are easy to grow and, like most herbs in the Labiatae family, can tolerate dry, poor soil. Although *L.angustifolia* is often referred to as English lavender, it, and most others, originate from Mediterranean areas. The aromatic oil and narrow, sometimes hairy leaves are part of their mechanism for survival in those hotter climates.

The traditional lavenders are basically made up of two tribes: there are forms of *L. angustifolia*, which include popular 'Hidcote', 'Munstead' and 'Loddon Pink',

LEFT
JEKKA'S FRONT GARDEN
Lavandula angustifolia with *L.* x *intermedia* 'Twickel Purple' in foreground

RIGHT
BERGAMOT
Monarda 'Squaw'

then there are numerous hybrids between *L. angustifolia* and *L. latifolia*, described as *L.* x *intermedia* cultivars. The latter are collectively referred to as Dutch lavender.

'If you want to grow a traditional type of lavender with strong fragrance, I would recommend *L.* x *intermedia* 'Seal,' said Jekka. 'It is tall, to about 90 cm (3 ft), with a haze of mid-purple flowers.' I ran my hand over its spikes; it really does have an intense perfume. '*L.* x *i.* 'Grappenhall' is another tall plant, this time with slightly paler flowers,' she said. 'For a smaller space, try *L.* x *i.* 'Twickel Purple', which reaches about 50 cm (20 in).'

Lavandula stoechas, or French lavender, is also popular. Compact at 60 cm (2 ft), it is grown for its short flowering stems topped by colourful purple bracts. I am less keen on its perfume, which reminds me of disinfectant. There is a pretty white form, *L. s.* f. *leucantha*. We looked at *L. s.* 'Marshwood', but like other tender kinds, it needs winter protection from extreme cold and damp. 'For a tough, showy French type of lavender, grow *L. stoechas* ssp. *pedunculata*,' advised Jekka. 'This Portugese native needs a sheltered position, but survives winter well in most gardens.'

Although I adore lavenders, my interest in herbs is mainly centred on their culinary uses. 'Look at this hyssop,' said Jekka. 'It is a classic labiate, with its pouting

ABOVE
FRENCH LAVENDER
Lavandula stoechas
'Marshwood'

RIGHT
THYME
Thymus pulegioides

FAR RIGHT
HYSSOP
Hyssopus officinalis

bottom lip and square stems. It was originally used as a cure for leprosy, because it makes an antiseptic wash. In cooking, it goes well with meat casseroles.' Next to it grew the beautiful bergamot, *Monarda* 'Squaw'. 'After the Boston Tea Party, the Oswego Indians provided monarda leaves for the white Americans to use as tea,' explained Jekka. 'It was used to flavour Earl Grey tea, but these days the oil comes from the bergamot orange. Monardas make good aromatic border plants, but need plenty of moisture to do well.'

One of Jekka's favourite herbs is *Satureja montana*. 'The winter savory is petite, smells good, has small white flowers and is excellent in cooking, because it helps break down food in the stomach,' she said. 'Anyone who has trouble with flatulence should try it.' As she spoke, I had dreams of once more being able to tackle artichoke soup. 'Oregano, too, is a good culinary herb and attracts many insects,' said Jekka. The small patch of herbs, fragrant under the hot sun, were indeed alive with bees, hoverflies and butterflies.

'The family cat is named Catmint, because she once ate a whole tray of it in the nursery,' Jekka recalled. '*Nepeta cataria* is the real catnip. Cats can get really high on it and few other types have the same effect.'

'Do you have problems with ants? Try pennyroyal (*Mentha pulegium*). Crush the leaves, wipe the sap along ant pathways, and it will send them away,' she said. 'This, like many herbs, should be taken with caution as it can be dangerous.'

Returning to culinary herbs, Jekka grows many thymes, including *Thymus pulegioides*. 'These are all edible, and like most herbs can be grown very successfully in pots. Use a well-drained, bark and peat compost and they will thrive. Basil does well in a pot too. He's probably the most difficult man you'll meet. Treat him well and never send him to bed with wet feet.' Joking apart, while the other herbs we examined are hardy perennials, the many different types of basil are tender annuals and should always be watered during the middle of the day.

Jekka has won many RHS Gold Medals and is in demand as an author and presenter, yet success will never stifle her love for herbs, or her desire to use them.

PERENNIAL SALVIAS AT WISLEY

Shrubby perennial salvias are great for brightening up late summer borders. They have a reputation for being tender, yet some can survive freezing winter temperatures outside. For a thorough investigation of the genus, botanist James Compton took Anne Swithinbank on a guided tour of the Salvia Trial at RHS Wisley.

DURING SUMMER the Portsmouth Field, Wisley, where trials are held, is essential viewing for anyone wanting to compare different species and cultivars within a plant group. Permanent trials of popular plants like dahlias and delphiniums are conducted every year; new cultivars are so numerous that regular assessments are important. Invited trials of other groups, including salvias, are held periodically. Jamie Compton, the country's leading expert on salvias, had been brought in to verify names in the trial, which had 236 entries.

Bringing all the salvias together means they can be compared and their names checked. There is also the opportunity for some of the plants to gain the coveted Award of Garden Merit (AGM). A committee decides on a set of criteria, then judges the plants. It is not the sort of competition to throw up one winner – there may be none or several awards given, depending on the standard of plants assessed. Buy a plant with AGM after its name and you should see good results.

Among the showiest of the perennial salvias is *S. patens* 'Cambridge Blue', which has already won an AGM. This has a height and spread of some 46–61 cm

LEFT
Salvia x *jamensis*
'James Compton'

RIGHT
BLUE SAGE
Salvia patens
'Cambridge Blue'

(18–24 in) and bears large, clear blue flowers. '*Salvia patens* comes from central Mexico, where it grows on damp banks,' said Jamie. 'One of the best, it survives cold weather by dying back to fleshy white tubers below ground. Fortunately it grows well in pots or tubs, which can be moved under cover for the winter in colder regions. Alternatively, the roots can be lifted and stored, rather like dahlia tubers.' My own plant, growing in well-drained soil, has survived -9°C (16°F).

'Salvias are easy to grow, being used to high meadows or dry rocky hillsides in the wild,' said Jamie. 'They like well-drained soil and most benefit from sheltered places where heat from the sun can build up. They are quite thirsty plants and the taller ones, in particular, need a lot of water as they are growing.'

We then admired some tall pink- and blue-flowered salvias, whose blooms were beautifully lit by the low rays of late summer sun. One of the most spectacular was *S.involucrata* 'Bethellii', which can reach 1.5 m (5 ft) tall. Shocking pink bracts enclose the slightly pouched, tubular purple-pink flowers, resembling big pink bubbles. The bracts fall away as the flowers open. Sadly, it does not tolerate frost well. 'Shoot-tip cuttings root easily,' said Jamie, 'and young plants can be overwintered in a frost-free greenhouse.'

Also capable of reaching 1.5 m (5 ft) is *S. guaranitica*, which has a wide distribution in South America. In the trial were several forms of this blue-flowered species. 'My favourite is 'Blue Enigma',' said Jamie. It produces its royal-blue flowers reliably and is the hardiest form, able to tolerate a minimum of -5°C (27°F). They are pollinated by humming birds, who thrust their beaks deep inside a flower to reach the nectar. This triggers the pollen-laden anthers, which drop pollen on to the bird's head to be carried to another flower.

One of the better-known of the shrubby salvias is *S. elegans*, the pineapple sage often grown in herb gardens. 'Sadly, this is more tender than some and needs

FAR LEFT
Salvia involucrata
'Bethellii'

LEFT
Salvia x *jamensis*
'La Luna'

RIGHT
PINEAPPLE SAGE
Salvia elegans

greenhouse protection during winter,' said Jamie. 'It is a good plant, though, with bright scarlet flowers and wonderfully aromatic, fruity-smelling leaves which are often used to flavour sponge cakes.' Cross-looking bees were hovering around the 1.8 m (6 ft) high clump. 'They would like to get to the nectar,' explained Jamie, 'but only humming birds are equipped to probe the flowers.'

Useful smaller salvias include *S. microphylla*, which reaches some 90 cm (3 ft) tall, and slightly shorter *S. greggii*. Both have dainty leaves and variable flower colours, mostly in shades of red and pink. Jamie visited Mexico with fellow botanists to observe and collect seed from some of these. 'In 1991, I went on a trip up into a high mountain plateau between the Sierra Madra Orientale and Sierra Madre Occidentale. We wanted to find the yellow-flowered form of *S. greggii*, which we did, above a little village called Jamé.'

At first, they found scarlet-flowered *S. greggii*, then, in shadier places, magenta-pink *S. microphylla*. 'As we continued, the colours of the salvias became more varied and we took seed from as many as 30 different shades of red, plum and pink. Finally, at around 1830 m (6,000 ft), we came across a clear sulphur-yellow and a lovely creamy colour.'

The botanists realized that most of the plants they were looking at were natural hybrids between the two species. Jamie subsequently named them *S.* x *jamensis* after the nearby village. One, *S.* x *j.* 'La Luna', was flourishing at Wisley. A lovely soft creamy yellow tinged with pink, it had been named after the Mexican moon. Coming from a high altitude, it is hardy to about -9°C (16°F).

Jamie says his interest in salvias will stay with him. 'I enjoy their huge variation and I will always want to grow them in my own garden.'

CHELSEA PHYSIC GARDEN

The Chelsea Physic Garden is perhaps one of London's best-kept secrets. Founded in 1673 by the Worshipful Society of Apothecaries of London, its 3.5 acres contain many Labiatae associated with medicinal use. In high summer, Anne Swithinbank visited the garden and met curator Sue Minter.

A S SUE AND I WALKED down an aromatic, lavender-lined path, the drone of London's incessant traffic receded. We arrived at a junction presided over by an impressive statue of Hans Sloane, who bought the manor of Chelsea from Charles Cheyne in 1712. 'It was Sloane who resurrected the garden after a period of decline and acted as its benefactor,' explained Sue. Apparently he is also famous for inventing the recipe for milk chocolate.

The Physic Garden became a very important botanic garden and was in continuous use by latter-day medical students. They would ring the old bell, which still hangs over Swan Walk gate, then enter to familiarize themselves with the plants they were to use in medicinal cures.

Salvia officinalis, or common sage, is one of them, and plants flourish in the warm, well-drained soil of the garden. 'Sage yields up essential oils widely used in perfumery, and also to flavour vermouth,' said Sue. 'To the Romans, it was a sacred herb, regarded as a heal-all. Infusions were used as mouthwashes and were gargled to clear sore throats.' These plants had been in bloom for several weeks, with some

LEFT
HIGH SUMMER IN CHELSEA PHYSIC GARDEN

RIGHT
CLARY SAGE
Salvia sclarea

lilac-blue flowers still showing. 'It's best not to let plants flower if you want a good succession of fresh leaves to use,' advised Sue. 'They become woody and age quickly, so it is best to prune them quite hard in spring'.

Sage is a small evergreen shrub, but close relative *Salvia sclarea* (clary sage) is biennial. The rosette of leaves that develops during the first year from seed produces spectacular spikes of shimmering cream and lilac flowers, 90 cm (3 ft) or more tall, during the second. 'It has an odd smell, doesn't it?' asked Sue, inviting me to touch the flower spikes and have a sniff. 'I've heard it referred to as sweaty Betty and hot housemaid.' Despite its rather astringent smell, it is used in aromatherapy. The oils it releases can have a sedative or uplifting effect and, as with all herbs, it should be used carefully. 'There is a story of a bunch of clary sage in a small car on a hot day,' said Sue. 'The oils volatilized and the driver emerged in quite a euphoric state – certainly not in a fit state to drive!'

The Chelsea Physic Garden has been open to visitors since 1983, but the atmosphere is far from museum-like. 'We still play an important part in research,' Sue explained. 'Dried plant material from the garden is being screened by two pharmaceutical companies for potential new drugs. Only some five per cent of the world's plants have been screened, so this is very important work. Especially at a time when habitats are threatened and species are becoming extinct before their properties can be evaluated.'

Not surprisingly, Sue's interest in the medicinal use of plants has grown since taking up the post as curator. 'Before this, I was Supervisor of the Palm House at

ABOVE
MINTBUSH
Prostanthera cuneata
'Fastigiata'

RIGHT
CULINARY SAGE
Salvia officinalis

Kew,' she said, 'and had already become fascinated with the many tropical plants used as medicine and food.' A degree in history prior to horticultural training has given her an almost ideal background for the job.

The soil in the Physic Garden is poor river-terrace gravel with no moisture-retaining subsoil. 'Before the embankment was built, the gardens lay alongside the Thames, so apothecaries could arrive by barge from the City of London,' she explained. 'The effect of the embankment, built in 1874, was to lower the water table to the point of being almost non-existent. Most of the herbs in Labiatae thrive in dry, poor soil, but for other plants we use huge quantities of organic matter. Within these walls is a unique microclimate and, without using protection, we can grow plants that would perish outside in most other parts of Britain.'

The pretty Australian mint bushes, prostantheras, fall into this category and, for labiates, bear quite large flowers. In a newly laid out area called the Garden of World Medicine, designed to show the use of plants in tribal medicine, Sue pointed out *P. cuneata*. The white flowers deserve close inspection, being decorated inside with purple and yellow markings, which mark out a runway for insects seeking nectar. 'This plant has a long history of use in Aboriginal medicine,' said Sue. 'Rub your hand gently along the shoots and it will come away smelling of menthol and camphor.' Not surprisingly, prostanthera has also been used as a decongestant. The neat bushes will reach up to 90 cm (3 ft) high, but need well-drained soil and protection from frost in all but the mildest areas.

As we completed our tour, I was struck by how remarkable the garden's survival has been. 'This is the only garden in Britain to have retained its original title of Physic after the old name for the healing arts.' said Sue. 'Today's interest in medicine combines with our national hobby of gardening and we are happy to invite people to see plants which may heal. I live here, and I can see how much they enjoy it!'

PLANTSMAN'S CHOICE

BILL CHUDZIAK

MOLUCCELLA LAEVIS, SALVIA VIRIDIS

Moluccella laevis is often called 'bells of Ireland', which is somewhat perplexing, as it comes from Syria. It is a half-hardy annual, with 60–90 cm (2–3 ft) branching flower spikes, and coarsely toothed leaves, typical of the salvia genus. The flowers, small and irrelevant, are carried in whorls, but each is cupped in a green papery calyx, and therein lies its ornamental value. The photographs in seed catalogues always make the plant look enticing, a chance escapee from a passing spacecraft, perhaps. In reality, the sprays of close-packed veined green saucers are quite mundane, and if I bothered to grow it again, it would probably be in the cutting garden. It is a great stalwart of flower-arranging, both in the green, and dried. The bracts dry well, turning a pleasant straw colour, silver-veined, and at this stage in their metamorphosis they appear more shell-like than floral. The Victorians loved skeletonizing plants, composing the results into pictures or arrangements to place under glass domes, and moluccella was a popular subject for this rather grisly hobby.

Salvia viridis, often mistakenly called clary, is another annual labiate grown for its bracts. These look like coloured leaves, so that each shoot appears tipped by purple, white, or dusky-pink tufts of foliage. In fact, these 'leaves' are true bracts sheltering tiny flowers.

LEFT
BELLS OF IRELAND *Moluccella laevis*

They are long-lasting and dry well, keeping their colour in winter arrangements. As a garden plant it has an old-world charm, and certainly both Gerard and Tradescant knew it and grew it. Doubtless it had medicinal properties, as the sages, above all, were valued as healing plants. This quotation taken from an early medicine text expresses the faith that physicians had in the genus: '*Cur morietur homo cui salvia crescit in horto?*': how can a man die who grows sage in his garden?

LAMIUM ORVALA

Many gardeners treat the lamiums like horticultural roughage. We all enjoy botanical equivalents of haute cuisine - exquisite waxy lilies, or swags of almond-scented clematis, plants which are exacting in their demands and often expensive to acquire. But there are areas of every garden where nothing seems to thrive. Gardeners look at the barren dry shade beneath trees, and immediately, unenthusiastically, think of lamiums – not very exciting, but utilitarian and reliable performers, just like branflakes.

This seems to me to be a shame, because the lamiums have immense charm, and are excellent mixers. The dead nettles are familiar roadside plants, and very pretty they can be, especially the marvellously named yellow archangel which grows alongside Lincolnshire ditches. This is *Lamium galeobdolon* (syn. *Galeobdolon luteum*), and although it has thuggish tendencies, it has given us

GIANT DEAD NETTLE
Lamium orvala

Ballota pseudodictamnus

WALL GERMANDER
Teucrium x *lucidrys*

LION'S EARS
Leonotis leonurus (syn. Leonotis ocymifolia)

CLARY
Salvia viridis syn. *S. horminum*

some first-rate garden forms. *Lamium galeobdolon* 'Hermann's Pride', an American cultivar, has a silvered leaf, but all the midribs and veins are picked out in green, so the foliage appears fretted. A well-grown spreading colony looks quite frivolously lacy. We have it slugging it out with purple ajuga, and the combination is terrific.

Much better mannered is *Lamium maculatum* and its many excellent cultivars. Most have very decorative foliage, exhibiting a silver flash along the centre of each leaf, like 'Chequers', or pink-flowered 'Roseum', or having a leaf which is entirely silver-frosted, like the much-grown 'Beacon Silver' or 'White Nancy'. *Lamium maculatum* 'Aureum' has a silver flash on gold foliage. All are undemanding, will make groundcover even in deep shade, or peep appealingly from underneath the petticoats of larger plants.

Lamium orvala is unusual in being grown principally for its flowers. These are large, tubular, and a lovely shade of copper pink. Damp killed it in our garden, but we intend to try again.

BALLOTA PSEUDODICTAMNUS

Ballota pseudodictamnus is a plant that I should dearly like to grow, but so far the mild, wet, west-of-Scotland climate has defeated all attempts. It comes from the sun-baked limestone hillsides of Crete, and is typical of the scrubby vegetation of the Mediterranean, being adapted to a rigorous life of starvation and oven-like temperatures. It makes a neat low mound of grey-green stems, woody at the base, and about 60 cm (2 ft) tall. Although it has a tendency to woodiness, it also regenerates by producing fresh growth from the base, herbaceous-style. It should properly be called a sub-shrub, along with other well-known Mediterranean plants like lavender, santolina or phlomis. The felty overcoat of woolly hairs which swathe the whole plant is a protection against the hot sun, a layer of insulation to keep cool, but they are also camouflage against browsing animals. The flowers, insignificant shreds of mauve, are borne in the leaf axils. They appear from small umbrella-shaped calyces which enlarge into furry seed vessels, and these, borne in whorls up the stem, provide the ornamental element which the flowers lack. 'All Hallows Green' is a selected form.

Ballota acetabulosa is a similar, but altogether bigger, plant from Greece, with larger calyces, lime-green in colour. The Greek name for the plant is '*louminia*', meaning light, as the funnel-like calyces were floated in olive oil, and then lit to provide a primitive oil lamp. Both plants are available to gardeners.

A well-drained hotspot is crucial for both ballotas, and doubtless they prefer a dash of limestone on the menu. They perform best in dry gardens, and are drought-tolerant. The future, complete with hosepipe bans is theirs. Ideal for the newly-fashionable gravel gardens, they will even tolerate impoverished rubble as a growing medium. A pane of glass would be a good idea if the winter is wet.

TEUCRIUM

There is a ruined cottage near Craigieburn which is scarcely more than a few piles of stones and the remains of a chimney wall. Nettles colonize the damp areas, but among the stones, where nothing else grows, are large numbers of *Teucrium* x *lucidrys*, known for centuries in our gardens as wall germander. It grows nowhere else around here, although the British native wood sage *Teucrium scorodonia* is common throughout the region. Wall germander is not an indigenous plant, having come originally from the Mediterranean, but it has been around for centuries, and inevitably, it has escaped and gone native. I like to think that it was grown and valued by the original cottager, and its tenacious clinging to the ruins is the last shred of a cottage garden before it is finally reclaimed by nature.

Wall germander is a quintessentially Elizabethan plant. They valued it greatly as one of the elements of the knot gardens which were then the height of horticultural fashion. Although these have often been recreated, they seldom contain the imaginative range of plants favoured by the Elizabethans, who did not confine themselves to box, but tried anything that would make a dwarf hedge; if it smelt good, like rosemary, santolina, or wall germander, then so much the better.

Rosemary Verey uses wall germander to great effect in her reinterpretation of a knot garden at Barnsley House in Gloucestershire. It is used in contrast with variously coloured box threads to create the effect of an over-and-under intertwining knot, enclosing domes of santolina and clipped box beehive shapes. Wall germander would also be the perfect plant with which to enclose blocks of herbs in a cottage garden. Clip it each spring to keep it dense and neat and to encourage the production of the mauvy pink-lipped flowers which appear in the leaf axils over the course of the summer.

LEONOTIS LEONURUS

In the last few years there has been a boom in the number of South African plants which have found their way into gardens. I had always assumed that *Leonotis leonurus* was a fairly recent introduction, and was amazed to learn that it was already here, growing under glass, in 1712.

This plant, which comes from grassy places and roadsides from Cape Province to Natal and Transvaal, is hardy in only the warmest gardens in Britain. It is a woody sub-shrub, although if cut down by frost, it will regenerate from the base, and it is worth trying in a sheltered garden, especially if you are prepared to give it a little

RIGHT
Leonotis leonurus (syn. *Leonotis ocymifolia*) white form

protection; bracken, straw, or agricultural fleece are ideal. The name means lion's ear, and the flowers are markedly furry.

In appearance it is a giant orange-scarlet dead nettle. The vivid whorls of tubular flowers are carried on somewhat gaunt woody stems which rise to 1.8 m (6 ft). The leaves are narrow and sparse, all the better to set off the showy tiers of bright flowers, which appear from October onwards in favoured areas. It might perhaps survive in mild northern gardens, but it is unlikely to make it into flower, so late in the year. This is a problem we in Scotland have with many South African plants. Species of schizostylis or watsonia thrive happily with us, but only manage to bloom in exceptionally long seasons. Fortunately, leonotis does well as a conservatory plant. If it spends the spring under protection it can stand out in the summer, and will flower earlier and make heartier plants than those which must struggle outside.

There is a white form which has recently come into general cultivation from Kirstenbosch Botanic Gardens. Novelty does not necessarily make something worth growing, and it is not half so showy as the scarlet type.

SALVIAS AND NEPETAS

Anne Swithinbank has written enticingly of some of the delectable South American salvias which lend such cachet to summer containers or conservatories (see pages 88–89). But there are other salvias, hardier and undemanding, that make distinctive and eye-catching border plants, sharing many of the characteristics of their more glamorous relatives. They tend to be first-rate 'fillers' for mixed planting schemes, and most have the desirable quality of enhancing neighbouring plants whilst giving a very good – and long-lasting – account of themselves. One absolutely classic high summer combination is *Salvia sclarea* var. *turkestanica* paired with old roses, particularly those in the crimson to grey-violet spectrum.

Salvia turkestanica is usually biennial, producing a flattish rosette of dark green wrinkled foliage throughout its first year. Its second year sees the emergence of great branched inflorescences bearing whorls of hooded flowers, bi-coloured greyish-lilac papery bracts, and this elegant and subtle melee of gentle colour is perfection with roses like 'Cardinal Richelieu' and 'Charles de Mills'. Unfortunately, there is nothing at all subtle about the aroma that it produces. Posh Edwardians called it 'Hot Housemaid', a term which measures at least nine on the Richter scale of political incorrectness, but this is highly evocative of those snobbish times when personal hygiene was so much easier for the rich. This salvia's best friend should tell it that it smells of stale sweat and mustiness, but do grow

LEFT
Phlomis longifolia

it anyway as it is a lovely and showy plant, and a reliable self-seeder.

Salvia concolor is one of my all-time favourite plants. It is a giant from Mexico which should, by rights, come into the half-hardy category. I have it growing in a shaded south-west facing border by the house, and every year I am sure I have lost it. In late May a few thin and unpromising shoots reappear, but by August these have rocketed up to 1.8 m (6 ft), producing robust square stems surrounded by an abundance of pale green foliage. Despite its feeble late start, when it comes to tidy the border in winter, we generally have to use shrub loppers on the mighty stems. The whorls of flowers, generously produced, are a clear vibrant navy blue, and the whole of the flowering stem has a bluish cast. It flowers away until felled by a sharp frost, and its only fault is a tendency to brittleness, so efficient staking is an absolute must. It is a stylish plant that should be better known.

Closely related to the salvias are the nepetas, popularly known as catmints. They, too, are evocative of the English style of gardening at its most effusive and romantic. *Nepeta* x *faassenii* is traditionally used as a billowing edge to borders of old roses or classic border plants like bearded iris or peonies. Shimmering borders of it are midsummer show-stoppers at gardens like Howick Hall in Northumberland or (of course) Hidcote. The plants are always full of drowsy bees, intoxicated by the essential oils, and the sound and scent of catmint on a sunny afternoon engenders great euphoria in most people. *Nepeta* 'Six Hills Giant' is even better, being twice as large as *Nepeta* x *faassenii* and, moreover, tolerant of a cool damp climate, so is ideal for northern gardens.

The best of all nepetas, though, is *Nepeta govaniana* from Kashmir. Unlike the sun-loving blues, this plant prefers cool moist conditions, and here, where conditions suit it, it reaches 1.4 m (4.5 ft). Open spikes of long-tubed flowers, pale clear yellow in colour, appear from July onwards. They are airy and delicate, and individual flowers seem to be attached by the merest thread, trembling delicately in the slightest breeze. The whole plant is, moreover, lemon-scented and long-flowering – an absolute star.

PHLOMIS

Recent hot dry summers have forced gardeners, particularly in the south, to go back to first principles. Instead of staring at brown borders and fawn lawns, they have turned to groups of plants that positively relish hot dry conditions. Many of these originate from the hot stony hillsides of the Mediterranean, a native habitat known as the *garigue*, and it is the particular realm of low-growing woody sub-shrubs such as cistus, artemisia and *Lavandula stoechas*.

Phlomis longifolia, from the eastern Mediterranean, has all the characteristics of a *garigue* shrub. Its tough felty leaves are immune to searing sunshine and the hot hairdryer winds which rake the exposed limestone cliff-faces of its native habitat. Members of the Labiatae family predominate in this type of vegetation, and the yellow hooded flowers of *Phlomis longifolia* are hooked and carried in tight whorls around the felty stems. The whole plant is rich in aromatic oils. Indeed, all the labiates are invariably alive with bees.

Phlomis italica, from the Balearics, is a particular favourite of mine. The foliage is grey and woolly, a wonderful foil for the cool porcelain-pink flowers. *Phlomis bovei* has showy bicoloured flowers of white overlaid with raspberry-pink. The flowers themselves are markedly felted, but the leaves are a somewhat dull plain green. All are desirable, though, and surprisingly easy to grow. They are marvellous subjects for the gravel gardens which are the fashionable pragmatic response to drought-ridden summers. In cooler wetter Scotland we sometimes lose them to winter wet, but like most labiates, they are ridiculously easy to root, so we always overwinter a pot of insurance cuttings. We grow them directly into a gravel

drive, where they thrive happily with rock roses and cistus, but a sunny spot and a shovelful of grit does just as well.

PHYSOSTEGIA

Physostegia is one of the many late-flowering perennials which hail from the United States. *Physostegia virginiana* was a fairly early transatlantic passenger, reaching our shores in 1683. Its introduction followed hard on the heels of the appointment of John Bannister as missionary to the American colonies. Within two years of his arrival in 1687, this keen young plantsman had compiled the first printed survey of American plants. He sent many good new introductions home, brought in through the Botanic Garden in Oxford where Bannister had been an undergraduate.

The name of the plant comes from the Greek *physa*, a bladder, and *stege*, roof covering, referring to fruits which are covered by an inflated calyx. However, it is familiarly known as the obedient plant

BELOW
Phlomis italica

because individual flowers can be moved to left or right on short hinged pedicels, a characteristic much enjoyed by children. Nobody seems to know why it has this strange ability. False dragonhead is its other name, and the open-mouthed, lipped flowers are somewhat reminiscent of heraldic dragon heads.

In the garden it makes a tidy and reliably floriferous clump about 90 cm (3 ft) in height. It is an obliging plant (obedient in every sense), which does not need staking and looks spry even after heavy rain. Its neat upright habit and medium height are useful contrasts to the tall undisciplined blousiness of many late flowering perennials. It is a good and upright citizen, somewhat lacking in glamour, but worthy of its place by virtue of being a good mixer. The type plant is pinky mauve, but there is a white form, and various cultivars. 'Summer Snow' is a shorter white and 'Bouquet Rose' a pale form. Garden writer Christopher Lloyd calls 'Vivid' 'a somewhat vicious rosy mauve', but uses it with characteristic aplomb. *Physostegia angustifolia* is similar, but harder to acquire.

STACHYS COCCINEA

Just about all gardeners know the silver-leaved carpeter, *Stachys byzantina*, usually known as 'lamb's ears' (or 'lugs' in Scotland). It forms a dense mat of woolly, silvered leaves and is almost a cliché used with old roses. But there are other stachys which make good garden plants, and one, which I am particularly fond of, is *Stachys coccinea*. This stachys is neither common nor utilitarian; it is quite rare in cultivation and needs a fair amount of cosseting. Originally from Mexico and Chile, it was introduced two hundred years ago.

From a mound of softly crinkled sage-green leaves emerge slender spires of long-tubed flowers on characteristically square stems. In reference books these flowers are generally referred to as scarlet, but the form that we grow is soft deep coral, a rare and beautiful colour among garden plants. The subtle harmony of leaf and flower is very satisfying, and although it does not make a huge horticultural splash, it is certainly a plant to be savoured and appreciated for its own sake.

So why, after two centuries, is not this lovely plant more widely grown? The answer lies in its dubious hardiness. We always make sure we have rooted cuttings as an insurance against winter loss, and there are usually a few replacement seedlings around any defunct parent plant. But how strange it is that gardeners will take cuttings as a matter of course for fuchsias, but pronounce it too much trouble for salvias or stachys.

Grow it in a well-drained warm spot in sun or partial shade. Best of all, give it a starring role as a specimen or container plant. It is intriguingly lovely with the sultry black velvet flowers of *Cosmos atrosanguineus,* from the same part of the world, or just on its own to admire and enjoy.

Phlomis bovei

THE OBEDIENT PLANT
Physostegia angustifolia

Stachys coccinea

THE
PEA
FAMILY

*Although legume is French for vegetable, this
family includes beautiful flowers as well as the
familiar pea. Even the runner bean, from Mexico,
was first grown as an ornamental. Others, from
temperate and tropical regions, have since graced
our flower borders and greenhouses.*

LEGUMINOSAE

FLOWER FACTS
THE BIRDS AND THE BEES

MOST OF OUR GARDEN legumes such as sweet peas, lupins, laburnums and wisterias, have typical pea-shaped flowers. They are often placed in the sub group Papilionoideae: with two lateral petals (wings), an upright dorsal petal (the standard), and two lower petals (the keel), they fancifully resemble butterflies. However, botany has more surprises; there are two other sub-groups. The Caesalpinoideae group contains flowers that can be distinguished by their five irregular petals, and these are very varied: those of the Judas tree are fairly similar to those in the papillion group, but those of the beautiful *Caesalpinia pulcherrima*, with five bright yellow petals and long red stamens, look more like rhododendrons than peas. The Mimosoideae group, with small five-petalled flowers arranged in pompoms, are easier to distinguish and include the ball-shaped yellow flowers of the acacias. The sub-groups are sometimes classed as three separate families: Papilionaceae, Caesalpiniaceae and yes, you've guessed it, Mimosaceae.

The fruits are more characteristic than the flowers. The seeds, from garden peas to leguminous trees, are carried in pods. *Delonix regia*, a stately tropical tree, has huge black pods up to 60 cm (2 ft) long. When these dry out they make amazing percussion instruments, and are known as mountain pianos in the Caribbean.

Many family members exhibit movement. French beans lower their leaves at night and raise them in the morning; sweet peas and wisteria have tactile tendrils that grow around whatever they touch. *Mimosa pudica*, the sensitive plant, goes even further: when touched, the leaflets and entire leaves collapse in seconds.

Many legumes can survive on poor soil as they can make their own fertilizer. Plants need nitrogen to grow, but have to absorb it through their roots as salts – inconvenient, when the surrounding air is over 78 per cent nitrogen! Legumes have found the answer. They team up with root bacteria called *Rhizobium* which converts nitrogen gas from the air into plant food. The relationship between plant and bacteria is symbiotic – both parties gain something from the other. In return for 'fixing' nitrogen gas into plant food, the bacteria are allowed to set up home by making root swellings, called nodules, and tapping into the plant's sugar supply.

When cut in half, a working nodule appears pink. This is due to a very rare phenomenon in the plant world – legumes can make blood. The enzyme that makes the plant food in the roots dislikes oxygen, but the roots need oxygen to breathe. The answer? Keep the oxygen in the roots, but away from the enzyme. The blood, called leghemoglobin, safely transports oxygen allowing it to reach only the parts where it is needed. So whatever you do, be sure to keep the vampire bats away from the beans!

WILD PEAS

THE PRIZE FOR THE BRIGHTEST and sweetest-smelling wild pea should go to *Ulex* species, the gorse. The common gorse (*Ulex europaeus*) covers hillsides with golden blossom from February to June, while the western gorse (*Ulex gallii*) flowers in late summer. Gorse smells fantastic: vanilla with a hint of pineapple, coconut and orange, all rolled into one. If the plant was not so prickly, it might have held a more prominent position in the garden border. Still, no matter, it looks so good untamed – and what better than a walk along a coastal path, with the scent of coconut wafting in the breeze?

Other shrubby wild peas include broom (*Cytisus scoparius*) and *Genista tinctoria*. Broom, found on heaths and waste ground, was actually used to make brooms in days gone by, and some people even regarded it as a magic shrub from which fairies would speak. *Genista tinctoria*, the dyer's greenweed, found throughout Europe and the eastern states of North America, still has a contemporary practical use. This small shrub, with its spikes of yellow flowers offset by bright green foliage, is used to make a yellow dye.

The perennial peas far outweigh the shrubby species, however. Rest harrow (*Ononis arvensis*) is a short perennial with beautiful pink pea flowers. Its common name perhaps derives from the experience of farmers, who could have thought the plant less attractive when its woody stems snared their harrows, causing them to rest! Maybe a donkey came to the rescue: *ono* means ass, and these creatures were supposed to be partial to the plant.

LEFT
GORSE
Ulex gallii 'Mizen Head'

One of our best-known and most varied wild legumes is the clover. In the red corner is red clover itself (*Trifolium pratense*), with white markings on its leaves, zigzag clover (*Trifolium medium*), crimson clover (*Trifolium incarnatum*) and strawberry clover (*Trifolium fragiferum*), whose dead flowers resemble strawberries (although to the eye, rather than to the taste buds!). In the white corner, apart from the typical white clover (*Trifolium repens*), which creeps along the ground, is rough clover (*Trifolium scabrum*), its small, egg-shaped flowers nestling next to the stem, and burrowing clover (*Trifolium subterraneum*), which buries its fruiting heads in the ground – a self-planting mechanism. Bees prefer white clover to red; it is more fragrant and the nectar is more accessible. It also secretes its nectar at lower temperatures than most other plants. The resulting honey is light amber and delicious. Red clover was once called 'honeysuckles' by country children as they, unlike the bee, could easily suck out the nectar by biting off the base of the flowers.

Lotus corniculatus, the bird's foot trefoil, has seed pods that resemble bird's feet. Other names include shoes and stockings, Tom Thumb, and bacon and eggs. The latter refers to the flowers which, with a little imagination, look the same colour as a traditional cooked breakfast!

Many native peas are climbers. Found throughout Europe, the vetches have flowers ranging from purple to yellow and use tendrils at their leaf tips to grab on to and climb up other plants. Although some people consider vetches to be weeds, *Vicia cracca*, the tufted vetch, with its spikes of blue and purple flowers clambering over the tops of hedges, is certainly a sight to behold from June through to August.

The wild relations of our much-loved sweet pea also use tendrils to climb. One of the most beautiful is the yellow *Lathyrus pratensis*, which scrambles over grassy hummocks. The sea pea (*Lathyrus japonicus*) is quite rare, confined to shingle beaches where it hugs the ground with creeping stems up to 80 cm (32 in) long, forming large patches of dark pink flowers. Although the garden sweet pea originated in Sicily, there are rumours that its yellow relation could be used in breeding programmes as, to date, there is no yellow sweet pea.

RIGHT
CRIMSON CLOVER
Trifolium incarnatum

WILD PEAS

KIDNEY VETCH
Anthyllis vulneraria

CROWN VETCH
Coronilla varia

BROOM
Cytisus scoparius

DYER'S GREENWEED
Genista tinctoria

HORSESHOE VETCH
Hippocrepis comosa

SEA PEA
Lathyrus japonicus

MEADOW VETCHLING
Lathyrus pratensis

BIRD'S FOOT TREFOIL
Lotus corniculatus

SAINFOIN
Onobrychis viciifolia

REST-HARROW
Ononis repens

STRAWBERRY CLOVER
Trifolium fragiferum

ALSIKE CLOVER
Trifolium hybridum

ZIGZAG CLOVER
Trifolium medium

RED CLOVER
Trifolium pratense

WHITE CLOVER
Trifolium repens

ROUGH CLOVER
Trifolium scabrum

BURROWING CLOVER
Trifolium subterraneum

COMMON GORSE
Ulex europaeus

WESTERN GORSE
Ulex gallii

TUFTED VETCH
Vicia cracca

THE FLOWERING YEAR

THE PEA YEAR starts with a bit of an outsider. The shamrock pea (*Parochetus communis*) boasts brilliant blue pea-shaped flowers that appear from October to February and, sporadically, throughout the summer. An evergreen perennial, this little ground-hugging plant requires a sheltered rock garden or preferably alpine house. *Acacia dealbata*, another late-winter flowering pea, also benefits from protection but is more suited to a sheltered south-facing wall as it can make a large shrub or small tree. Its fragrant yellow pompom flowers are well known as the florist's mimosa. *Sophora microphylla* 'Sun King', which flowers at the same time, has more typically pea-shaped yellow flowers and withstands a bit more cold. *Lathyrus vernus*, a perennial relation of the sweet pea, comes into flower in March. Named the spring pea, it is hardy and comes in blue, pink, purple and white. It can attain a height of 40 cm (16 in) and looks good positioned at the front of a border or climbing through a shrub rose.

The yellow gorse starts the ball rolling for the profusion of spring-flowering woody peas. *Coronilla valentina* subsp. *glauca* is a firm favourite, with its clusters of rich yellow flowers smelling of ripe peaches. The early-flowering broom, *Cytisus* x *praecox*, is later followed by *C. scoparius,* with colours ranging from yellow and chocolate to suffused pink. April and May bring the golden flowers of laburnum and piptanthus, the evergreen laburnum, the blue and mauve chains of wisteria and the branch-hugging pink blossoms of the exquisite Judas tree.

MARCH

SOPHORA
Sophora microphylla
'Sun King' (HS)
March–May

COMMON GORSE
Ulex europaeus (HS)
March–May

APRIL

CORONILLA
Coronilla valentina subsp.
glauca (HS)
April (and sporadically
through the year)

WARMINSTER BROOM
Cytisus x *praecox* (HS)
April–May

COMMON BROOM
Cytisus scoparius (HS)
April–May

GOLDEN RAIN TREE
Laburnum anagyroides (HT)
April–July

MAY

★FAIRY DUSTER
Calliandra eriophylla (HHS)
May–September

★★JUDAS TREE
Cercis siliquastrum (HT)
May–June

LOBSTER CLAW
Clianthus puniceus (HHWC)
May–June

MEADOW VETCHLING
Lathyrus pratensis (HP)
May–August

LUPIN
Lupinus (Russell Hybrids) (HP)
May–July

MOON TREFOIL
Medicago arborea (HS)
May–October

EVERGREEN LABURNUM
Piptanthus nepalensis (HS)
May–June

CHINESE WISTERIA
Wisteria sinensis (HS/HWC)
May–June

KEY
★ from the Mimosoideae group
★★ from the Caesalpinoideae group
All other species are from the Papilionadeae group.
A: annual B: biennial P: perennial S: shrub
HH: half-hardy H: hardy T: tree
WC: woody climber

JUNE

FALSE INDIGO
Baptisia australis (HP)
June

CAESALPINIA
★★*Caesalpinia decapetala* var.
japonica (HHS)
June

YELLOW WOOD
Cladrastis lutea (HT)
June

BLADDER SENNA
Colutea arborescens (HS)
June–September

COMMON CORAL TREE
Erythrina crista-galli (HHS)
June–July

GOAT'S RUE
Galega offininalis (HP)
June–July

INDIGOFERA
Indigofera heterantha (HS)
June–September

SWEET PEA
Lathyrus odoratis (HA)
June–September

PARROT'S BEAK
Lotus berthelotii (HHP)
June–September

★SENSITIVE PLANT
Mimosa pudica (HHA)
June–September

BLACK LOCUST
Robinia pseudoacacia (HT)
June

WHITE CLOVER
Trifolium repens (HP)
June–September

JULY

WESTERN GORSE
Ulex gallii (HS)
July–November

AUGUST

LIQUORICE
Glycyrrhiza glabra (HP)
August–September

FRENCH HONEYSUCKLE
Hedysarum coronarium (HHB/P)
August–September

SENNA
★★*Senna corymbosa* (H/HHS)
August–September

SEPTEMBER

AMICIA
Amicia zygomeris (HHS)
September–November

JAPANESE PAGODA TREE
Sophora japonica (HT)

OCTOBER

SHAMROCK PEA
Parochetus communis (HP)
October–February

DECEMBER

★MIMOSA
Acacia dealbata (H/HHT)
December–March

Tree peas carry on into the summer with the stunning yellow flowers of the bladder senna (*Colutea arborescens*) and yellow wood (*Cladrastis lutea*), better known for its yellow autumn colour. However, now the main stage is for the herbaceous peas. Galegas in white and mauve brighten up the back of the border, fronted by the violet-blue flowers of baptisia and spires of lupins in every colour and shade. Sweet peas bring a splash of colour to fences, walls and shrubs, and pink and mauve clambering, perennial lathyrus and yellow tree lupins increase the range.

Scarlet peas add a real hot spot. In a warm, sheltered area, the semi-evergreen, scrambling climber *Clianthus puniceus*, aptly named lobster claw. For something a little smaller, grow the trailing red pea, (*Lotus berthelotii*), in a summer basket or over a small wall.

More shrubs appear in late summer and autumn. In a sheltered spot *Senna* x *floribunda* produces sprays of bowl-shaped, rich yellow flowers. *Calliandra haematocephala* with its large red powder-puff flowers, is even more tender and requires the protection of a heated glasshouse. Its relation, *Calliandra eriophylla*, also tender, flowers from late spring to autumn and is descriptively known as the fairy duster. *Amicia zygomeris* is the last stand for outdoor tree peas, and tries to bring its yellow flowers to bloom before the first frosts.

PEA DIRECTORY

TYPE OF PLANT	(H) HEIGHT (S) SPREAD	CONDITIONS REQUIRED (SEE KEY)	PLANT TYPE AND CULTIVATION TIP	PROPAGATION
ACACIA				
Acacia dealbata	**H** 9 m (30 ft) **S** 3 m (10 ft)	○☼❋	Tree. Plant in sheltered spot.	Seed.
Acacia pravissima	**H** 1.8 m (6 ft) **S** 90 cm (3 ft)	○☼❋	Tree. Plant in sheltered spot.	Seed.
Amicia zygomeris	**H** 1.8 m (6 ft) **S** 1.8 m (6 ft)	○☼❋	Herbaceous perennial. Plant in sheltered spot.	Cuttings all year round.
Cercis siliquastrum	**H** 8 m (25 ft) **S** 6 m (20 ft)	○☼❋	Tree. Do not transplant.	Seed or cuttings.
Galega officinalis 'Alba'	**H** 90 cm (3 ft) **S** 1.5 m (5 ft)	○◑☼❋❋	Herbaceous perennial. Stake.	Seed or division.
Indigofera heterantha	**H** 3 m (10 ft) **S** 1.8 m (6 ft)	○☼❋❋	Shrub. Cut out dead wood in spring.	Seed or soft wood cuttings.
Laburnum anagyroides	**H** 4.5 m (15 ft) **S** 3 m (10 ft)	○◑☼◐❋❋❋	Tree. Avoid waterlogged sites.	Seed.
LATHYRUS				
Lathyrus niger	**H** 90 cm (3 ft) **S** 90 cm (3 ft)	○☼◐❋❋❋	Herbaceous perennial. Mulch with compost in spring. Watch for aphids.	Sow seed in spring. Divide roots and replant in spring.
Lathyrus odoratus	**H** 1.8 m (6 ft) **S** 45 cm (18 in)	○☼◐❋❋	Annual climber. Provide support. Dead head regularly. Control aphids.	Sow seed in spring.
Lathyrus tingitanus	**H** 1.2 m (4 ft) **S** 45 cm (18 in)	○☼◐❋❋	Annual. As above.	Sow seed in spring.
Lathyrus vernus 'Albòroseus'	**H** 45 cm (18 in) **S** 45 cm (18 in)	○☼◐❋❋❋	Deciduous perennial. Mulch with compost in spring. Watch for aphids.	Sow seed in spring. Divide roots and replant in spring.
Lathyrus x tubro	**H** 1.5 m (5 ft) **S** 75 cm (30 in)	○☼◐❋❋❋	Deciduous perennial climber. Mulch with compost in spring. Provide support. Control aphids.	Divide roots in spring. Basal cuttings in spring.

Lotus berthlottii	**H** 60 cm (2 ft) **S** 60 cm (2 ft)	◊ ☼ ☀ ✹	*Tender perennial.* *Protect over winter.*	*Cuttings.*
Lupinus littoralis	**H** 15 cm (6 in) **S** 60 cm (2 ft)	◊ ☼ ✹✹✹	*Alpine perennial.* *Dead head.*	*Seed or cuttings.*
Lupinus 'Aston Villa', *L.* 'Red Arrow' *L.* 'Canary Bird'	**H** 90 cm (3 ft) **S** 60 cm (2 ft)	◊ ☼ ☀ ✹✹✹	*Deciduous herbaceous* *perennial.* *Best planted young.* *Guard against slugs* *and lupin aphid.*	*Basal cuttings in* *mid-spring.*
Strongylodon macrobotrys	**H** 18 m (60 ft) **S** 3 m (10 ft)	◊ ◖ ☼ ✹	*Evergreen, tropical* *climber 16°C (min 64°f).* *Leave it to the experts!*	*Seed when available.*
Wisteria sinensis	**H** 6 m (20 ft) **S** 6 m (20 ft) plus	◊ ◖ ☼ ✹✹✹	*Deciduous woody climber* *Shrub.* *Prune after flowering* *and again in late* *winter.*	*Seed occasionally but* *grafted is best.*

KEY

◊ Well drained soil ◖ Moist soil ● Wet soil ☼ Sun ☀ Partial shade ✹ Tolerates full shade
✹ Half-hardy to 0°C (32°F) ✹✹ Frost-hardy to -5°C (23°F) ✹✹✹ Fully hardy to -15°C (5°F)

THE GARDENS
RUSSELL LUPINS

When he was sixteen, Johnny Walker cycled past a field of Russell lupins and was so amazed by their colours, he nearly fell off his bike. This was the start of a lifetime's fascination with both the plants and their breeder, George Russell, a complex character who almost kept his strain of lupins a secret from the world.

A PURPLISH BLUE-FLOWERED SPECIES, *Lupinus polyphyllus*, reached Britain from the American west coast in 1826. Early hybridization created rather weak shades of blue, white, pasty yellow and later, rose-pink. George Russell, born near York in 1857, was working as a jobbing gardener when he noticed these rather inferior lupins, and decided they had great potential. During the 1920s and 1930s, Russell settled down to serious lupin breeding; he used several different species in addition to the existing hybrids, and weeded out bad plants before the bees could pollinate other flowers. He refused to sell his plants and destroyed any paperwork pertaining to them. The only person he trusted with his secrets was his young assistant, Arthur (Sonny) Heard.

The field that Johnny cycled past in the early 1950s belonged to James Baker, owner of a nursery at Codsall, near Wolverhampton. Baker had finally persuaded the 80-year-old Russell to sell him his lupins, so that they could live on. With the lupins came Sonny, who knew the plants and processes of selection inside out.

LEFT
JOHNNY WALKER'S LUPINS

RIGHT
LUPIN
Lupinus 'Aston Villa'

The gardening world was shown Russell lupins for the first time at the Royal Horticultural Society's June show in 1935, when the clear, bright colours and stems tightly packed with chunky blooms caused a sensation.

After leaving the RAF, Johnny remembered the field of lupins, managed to find Baker's nursery and bought a good stock. 'When I heard the nursery was going downhill fast, I bought as many named varieties as I could, and befriended Sonny.'

When I visited Johnny, he showed me the square plot where he now keeps his lupins. 'I used to have a small field and could grow about a thousand at a time,' he said. 'Now, I am restricted to fifty, most of which I have bred myself.' Like Russell, he rogues out undesirable plants, collecting seed only from the best. 'They say alike as two peas in a pod,' he said, 'but every seed is different. I can only grow a tiny percentage, and wonder about the missed potential in those I'll never see.'

Many of Johnny's varieties have been successful. 'A good lupin should have a well-rounded bell petal at the front, with a flat standard at the back, and the flowers should be packed together so that no stem is visible between them,' he explained. 'I also look for spikes capable of opening right up to the top before the lowest flowers start dying off.' Yellow 'Canary' showed all these good points, as did nearby 'Aston Villa', an alluring mix of blue, tinged with a warm mauve.

We admired the colour range, including dramatic reds, and purples like 'Twilight', whose dark flowers are suffused with warm maroon at the top, but acquire yellow markings as they age. Johnny always keeps good plants for three years to let them develop their true nature: 'I nearly threw 'Canary' away after a year, because it looked weak,' he said, 'but look at it now.'

LEFT
Lupinus 'Red Arrow'
Lupinus 'Canary'

RIGHT
JOHNNY WALKER'S LUPINS

Lupins like a lime-free, slightly acid soil, well-drained and not too rich. They must be protected against slugs, and may need spraying against the giant lupin aphid. This looks like a monster, but is quickly cleared up by spraying with a pirimicarb-based product. 'Lupins like a slight slope and an open position away from any overhanging trees,' said Johnny. 'Plant while still quite young,' he said, 'so they can put down a good deep root system.'

Lupin seed usually germinates easily. 'I rub seeds together gently between sand paper to wear down the hard seed coat, which lets water in faster,' he explained. 'I sow in spring, into trays of John Innes seed compost in the greenhouse or coldframe. After germination they are moved outside. Seedlings are pricked out into small pots, or sometimes straight into the ground.'

Good hybrids are bulked up by division or cuttings, taken in early spring. Shoots 8 cm (3 in) long are removed by cutting them so low down, they often have roots attached. Inserted around the edges of pots filled with a 50:50 mix of peat and sharp sand, they are kept outdoors, but shaded from hot sun. By late spring, they have rooted and can be potted separately, then planted out soon after. It pays to propagate lupins regularly, as they tend to be short-lived.

I wondered what Johnny's favourite colour was. 'I used to like pillarbox-red, but now it's good, strong blues,' he said. This flies in the face of Russell's criteria, whereby blues were rejected because they were too close to wild lupins. 'I am concerned about the future of Russell lupins,' Johnny confessed. 'I let a seed company have seeds from my plants, and friends own a nursery selling named varieties.' Occasionally, he will add one of their plants to his pool of excellence. 'If a keen young grower came forward, I would willingly set them up with plants and encouragement,' he said. 'Like Russell, I think lupins have still more to offer.'

THE LATHYRUS GARDEN

Sylvia Norton's cottage garden in Cambridgeshire provides a framework for the National Collection of lathyrus. These dainty cousins of the sweet pea are often eclipsed by their showier relative, but Anne Swithinbank found their pretty flowers delightful.

ALWAYS AN ADMIRER of the sweet pea, Sylvia Norton became captivated by the wilder kinds in 1984, when she bought a plant of *L. vernus,* the spring pea. In a short time, she found herself holder of the National Collection, with all its attendant responsibilities. From a gardening point of view, the important attributes of these peas include whether they are annual or perennial, and then whether they climb or not. There is a variety of choice in each category and all are easy to grow. Among the annual climbers are some striking species which offer a quick solution to bare vertical surfaces in the garden. It seems apt to talk about *Lathyrus odoratus* first, because this bicolored magenta and purple ancestor of the sweet pea has been responsible for many a row of colourful, frilly-petalled, large-flowered modern hybrids. As its name suggests, it is about as sweet-smelling as a pea can get. Although introduced from Sicily some 300 years ago, it was the end of the nineteenth century before Henry Eckford, the 'father of the sweet pea', embarked upon his legendary breeding programme. First came the Grandiflora

LEFT
SPRING PEA
Lathyrus vernus
'Alboroseus'

RIGHT
SWEET PEA
Lathyrus odoratus

LEFT
TANGIER PEA
Lathyrus tingitanus

RIGHT
BLACK PEA
Lathyrus niger

FAR RIGHT
Lathyrus x *tubro*
(Lathyrus tuberosus x
Lathyrus rotundifolius)

strain, with flowers much larger than any of the wild peas. They were superseded in 1901, when variants with waved petals appeared simultaneously among the collections of Silas Cole (head gardener at Althorp Park) and of W. J. Unwin. One was named 'Countess Spencer', and gave rise to the modern Spencer type of sweet pea we all enjoy today.

Despite the showiness of modern hybrids, I agreed with Sylvia that *L. odoratus* was worth growing for its simple beauty and fragrance. 'In the Collection, I have what is thought to be the original form of the species, as well as some of the oldest cultivars,' she said. 'I sow in October, because nature sows her seeds then, but, in case of winter fatalities, I also set six to eight seeds to a pot in spring.' They end up in large pots of good growing compost fitted with supports which Sylvia weaves herself, using long narrow stems of basket-maker's willow. 'They cling with their tendrils and need little help,' said Sylvia, 'but dead heading is essential with all the annual climbers, to keep more flowers coming.' This style of growing is ideal for sunny patios and balconies.

Other handsome annual climbers include the Tangier pea, *L. tingitanus*. Its bright pink, pointed flowers are full of character, appearing during the first part of summer on plants whose winged stems climb to 1.2 m (4 ft) or more. Sylvia also grows *L. sativus* var. *azureus*, the Turkish chickling pea. 'This is often grown as a fodder crop, but beware, as the seeds are poisonous,' she said. 'It gets confused with Lord Anson's blue pea *(L. nervosus)*, but the flowers are carried singly on the stem, and are a beautiful sky blue. Lord Anson's pea bears flowers that are the mauve-blue of periwinkles, in whorls of three or four up the stems, and is perennial.'

Growers of sweet peas for exhibition have their own particular methods of producing long-stemmed blooms, but all the annual climbers can be easily grown in the open soil. 'I sow 10-15 seeds in one pot, then plant them out together near a support,' said Sylvia. 'A good bucketful of compost in the planting hole and water during droughts are all they need to flower over several months.'

For gardeners who do not want to sow seeds every year, there are good perennial climbers. Probably the best known is the broad-leaved everlasting pea *(L. latifolius)*, which bears scentless purple-pink, pale pink or white flowers all summer and can often be seen on roadsides and railway embankments.

In Sylvia's garden, the rich pink flowers of *L.* x *tubro* caught my eye. These, too, have no perfume. However, Sylvia knows how to use her plants, and had cunningly sited her *L.* x *tubro* to scramble through sweet rocket, and then up into the shrubby heights of rose 'Blanc Double de Coubert'. A clever planting scheme combining colours and perfumes to best effect. 'I rather like the mixture of new buds and open blooms,' commented Sylvia. 'This pea dies back for winter, but I don't cut away the foliage, because I believe it protects the plant.'

Other perennials make good clumps, but do not climb. *L. vernus*, the spring pea, will reach a height and spread of only some 45 cm (18 in). In the wild, it brightens forest, scrubland and rocky ledges with its purple flowers, which fade to blue as they age. It is equally resilient in gardens. In Sylvia's, it was also represented by its lovely soft pink and white-flowered form, *L. v.* 'Alboroseus'. The tiny flowers of vetch-like *L. niger*, the black pea, need close examination to appreciate the attractive markings on blooms essentially a purple shade, fading to blue. This small, bushy plant, which can reach 90 cm (3 ft) tall, gets its name because all its parts turn black as they die.

The perennial peas are even easier to grow than annual peas. 'Mulch them with compost in spring,' advised Sylvia, 'but once established they become quite drought tolerant and will not even need dead heading.' All the peas, but particularly the annuals, are susceptible to aphids. 'This need not be a problem if you patrol regularly with soft soap at the ready,' said Sylvia, 'then the situation never gets out of control.' Growing her peas and keeping up with the paperwork associated with any National Collection keeps Sylvia busy. An important task is seed collection. 'At the moment, I don't produce a catalogue, but I can supply seed to those who ask,' she stated. 'The whole point of maintaining a collection is to spread your plants around, so more gardeners can try them.'

PLANTSMAN'S CHOICE

BILL CHUDZIAK

ACACIA

In the eighteenth and nineteenth centuries, Britain became increasingly outward-looking, and hard on the heels of the explorers came the botanists. Perhaps the greatest of these was plant hunter and botanical entrepreneur, Sir Joseph Banks. Although his passion for plants ranged worldwide, the flora of the Pacific, and particularly Australasia, was his special province. We have Banks to thank for the acacias, from Australia and Tasmania, still rare in gardens, despite being introduced nearly two centuries ago.

The acacias are in their own section of the Leguminosae called the Mimosoideae. They differ from the rest of the family in having distinctly unpea-like fluffy yellow balls for flowers, the best-known being the vanilla-scented florist's mimosa. *Acacia pravissima*, or Oven's wattle, is occasionally seen in mild Cornish gardens, where

it seems reasonably reliable. It comes from south-east Australia where it wages a constant battle with arid heat and browsing animals. It has adapted to the blistering heat by producing tough flattened alternative leaves called phyllodes, each tipped by a vicious spine to deter would-be munchers. In some species, pinnate leaves coexist with the phyllodes. To protect against sunburn, all the foliage has a silvery-blue cuticle, almost like a coat of protective wax. Most acacias have this adaptation, and very decorative it is too. E. A. Bowles, a great garden writer, described *Acacia baileyana* as having 'leaves as blue as a freshly-killed mackerel.'

Like many tender shrubs, acacias are fast-growing, so several consecutive mild winters will see them established and, even if frosted, they will sprout from the base. They are not lime-tolerant, so an acid soil is *de rigueur*. So if you live in Cornwall or Killarney, give the acacias a go; otherwise, leave them alone. Nothing is worse than a tender plant that merely survives, stunted and miserable, unable to fulfil its splendid potential.

WISTERIA

Wisteria is, perhaps, the grandest climber in cultivation. It originates in Japan, growing wild in deep forests, but the forms we grow in our gardens are far removed from the wild. The Chinese and Japanese value wisteria highly, and for centuries their nurseries have patiently bred and selected the most beautiful forms. They are as much the outcome of oriental civilization as a Ming vase or lacquer screen, and, moreover, they are available to us all.

We grow mainly *Wisteria floribunda*, from Japan, or *Wisteria sinensis*, from China. The former, especially in the variety *W. f.* 'Macrobotrys,' has exceptionally long racemes of violet-blue flowers, whilst the latter is more floriferous and headily scented. Curiously, the Japanese wisteria twines clockwise, the Chinese, anti-clockwise. There are other species, and also some magnificent selections and hybrids: white-flowered sports, doubles, and varieties with parti-coloured flowers. But none is quite so evocative of balmy early summer evenings as the old-fashioned mauve varieties.

FAR LEFT
Acacia dealbata

LEFT
Acacia pravissima

Wisteria sinensis

JUDAS TREE
Cercis siliquastrum

GOLDEN CHAIN TREE
Laburnum anagyroides

Taking on a wisteria is quite a commitment. Fertile soil and careful site preparation are essential. A warm wall is usually the chosen site, but *Wisteria floribunda* is better on a pergola or arch, where the foot-long racemes can hang free.

Pruning and training need a level head. The plant has the capacity to ramp to 30 m (100 ft), but is quite amenable to drastic curbing. The object is roughly analogous to fruit-tree pruning: limit vegetative growth to promote flower production. The huge whip-like summer shoots look daunting, but in early August, simply cut them back to 15 cm (6 in), encouraging the production of flowering spurs. In winter, prune them again to 7-10 cm (3-4 in), leaving only two or three buds on each spur.

The Victorians loved to train wisteria into elaborate arbours, and even used it to create living gazebos. These must have looked beautiful, but anyone sheltering from the sun would have been in danger from drunken bees dropping from the roof, as wisteria is always alive with the murmur of working bees. In Cambridge Botanic Gardens we were privileged to see a grove of wisteria painstakingly trained into 1.8 m (6 ft) tall multi-stemmed standards, each a shimmering fountain of blossom. The scent on a hot June day was intoxicating, and I was bowled over by the skill of the gardeners who had created and cared for these marvellous specimens. For a well-trained mature wisteria is a sign of a serious garden. The gnarled framework of branches is splendid and full of character even in the depths of winter, and in full flower, it is one of the most glorious and sensual sights of summer.

CERCIS

I was lost in Granada when I first encountered *Cercis siliquastrum*, the Judas tree. A wrong turn had led me into a labyrinth of narrow streets, eventually opening out into a small dusty square where scrawny cats dozed in the sun and scarlet pelargoniums spilled out of old olive oil cans. In one corner was a Judas tree in full glorious flower, and I was utterly entranced.

A native of the eastern Mediterranean, it reached England in the sixteenth century, but my guess is that it has been in Spain for much longer. The Moors, who laid out the courtyards and gardens of Granada, surely knew it and used it. Traditionally, it was the tree upon which Judas Iscariot hanged himself, causing it to blush rosy-pink with shame; a dour legend for such a heart-lifting plant.

Ultimately it reaches about 8 m (25 ft), neat when young, but snaking and layering itself when mature and allowed its lebensraum. The leaves are beautiful, kidney-shaped and smooth. They are lightly rimmed with maroon, and have a clammy texture, as if hanging on to every nanodrop of moisture. The extravagant clusters of rosy-mauve pea-flowers pre-empt the leaves, garlanding the bare branches with exuberance – in full bloom it is as showy and exotic as any tropical legume. The flowers have the eccentric habit of appearing directly from old wood, even springing irreverently from gnarled and venerable trunks.

Cercis needs sun and wind to ripen the wood for flowering. It is a common street tree in Spain and Portugal, and the strong blue of a Mediterranean sky sets off the blossom to perfection. It succeeds best in the south and east of Britain, needing a south wall in cooler wetter parts. Root disturbance is anathema, so do not move it. It is, however, amenable to training, so if you have a warm garden, and want an alternative to the ubiquitous laburnum, try an espalier walk, or even a tunnel, of the lovely Judas tree.

LABURNUM

Laburnum anagyroides, the common laburnum, must be one of the most familiar trees in Britain. Just about every street in the country that has gardens plays host to at least one laburnum. It comes from south and central Europe and has been around our gardens since the sixteenth century. A second species, *Laburnum alpinum*, known as the Scotch laburnum, is later-flowering, has longer racemes, and is rather more handsome. Both are bone hardy and dead easy to grow, being completely unchoosy as to soil or position. The only drawback is that all parts of laburnum are highly toxic, so vigilance is required if young children are around.

There has been a terrific vogue recently for laburnum tunnels, and very handsome they look lit up with the long pendent racemes of golden flowers. But to my mind, their season of glory is a short one, and they have no special beauty of leaf or form, nor autumn colour, to enliven such a planting for the rest of the summer.

I like laburnum best in a natural setting. They have escaped in many places and, growing on the fringes of natural woodland, are transformed. The first flowers come just as native trees have leafed up and are at their most ravishing, and the airy yellow blossom seems to intensify the freshness of spring.

A chimera is a plant that is a graft hybrid of two different species. +*Laburnocytisus adamii* is such a chimera, being *Cytisus purpureus* grafted onto *Laburnum anagyroides*. Some branches have yellow racemes, some purple broom flowers, whilst others have brown intermediate flowers. Some people adore this curiosity, but I feel that just because a thing can be done does not mean it should be done. To me it is an aberration – I prefer my laburnum *au naturel*.

STRONGYLODON MACROBOTRYS

Most gardeners think of the pea family as being utilitarian, grown for their food value (peas and beans), as cut flowers (sweet peas), or

RIGHT
JADE VINE *Strongylodon macrobotrys*

as the cast-iron stalwarts of the garden (lupins or laburnum). But a huge proportion of this diverse family is to be found in the tropics, and among them are many beautiful, intriguing, or downright peculiar plants.

The jade vine stops you in your tracks. It flourishes in the steamy heat of the Philippine jungle, where the thickness of the tree canopy keeps the light levels low. So exuberant is the vegetation here that competition for survival is fierce, and climbers, epiphytes and saplings elbow each other aside in their race towards the light.

Its Latin name is *Strongylodon macrobotrys*, which means, quite literally, big racemes of curved teeth, and this describes pretty accurately its hanging clusters of fang-like flowers. These are an extraordinary colour, an unearthly luminous blue-green, more mineral than vegetable. They look like the flora of another planet, and in a sense this is apt, as the jungle is its own world, in many ways as strange and remote as another universe.

The jade vine is principally pollinated by humming birds. The soft luminosity of the flowers, possibly enhanced by high ultra-violet content, allows the pollinator to recognize them in the gloom of the deep forest. It needs a minimum temperature of 64° F (18° C) and sky-high humidity. It also has the potential to grow to 18 m (60 ft), so it is not really feasible for the conservatory. Threatened in the wild by the march of so-called civilization, it thrives happily in many botanic gardens where its conservation is assured. Pay it an annual visit in late spring when it is in full flowering glory. Wonderful, spectacular, breathtaking? Yes, of course. But is it beautiful? Decide for yourself.

GALEGA OFFICINALIS

Goat's rue, *Galega officinalis*, is one of those old-fashioned plants that is easily overlooked when planning a border. However, to say that it resembles a giant vetch certainly does not do it justice, and makes it sound a great deal less exciting than it is. It forms loose clumps about 90 cm (3 ft) tall of delicate pinnate foliage in a good fresh green. The sheaves of pretty pea flowers, copiously produced, do not overwhelm the plant, but are presented in just the right leaf-to-flower ratio. It is surprising how few plants manage to pull this trick off, and many sought-after border perennials lack the graceful equilibrium of galega. Sometimes the flowers are a rather greyish mauve, but in the best forms they are lilac, lavender, or rosy mauve. These forms are usually listed as *Galega* x *hartlandii*, and there are also some named varieties, which can be difficult to get hold of. The white form is very special, particularly at twilight.

A midsummer trip visiting West Country gardens introduced me to the virtues of this plant, and I returned with several good forms to begin stocking my own borders. In great and quintessentially English gardens like Hidcote in Gloucestershire and Tintinhull in Somerset, galega spills its blue-mauve or white flowers through the roses and delphiniums of high summer. It is a wonderful filler, inveigling itself into vacant nooks and crannies, softening the emphatic verticals of verbascums, discreetly concealing the gaunt lower limbs of shrub roses with a flounce of mauve-pink. In the flat bright afternoon light at Tintinhull a planting of galega, coreopsis and artemisia, backed with philadelphus and hemmed with blue viola, looked like an impressionist painting – busy but harmonious.

Galega is a plant that is very easy to grow, as it requires only full sun and reasonably good drainage. It will manage to thrive on even the poorest of soils, and is drought-tolerant. All in all, galega is a plant ripe for rediscovery.

AMICIA ZYGOMERIS

This large and handsome pea is for gardeners who enjoy choice curiosities. *Amicia zygomeris* comes from western Mexico, so it is for warm gardens or cool conservatories, but it is a real eyecatcher and well worth a bit of mollycoddling.

The stout hollow stems are covered with a velvety down, rather like those of *Rhus typhina*, the well-known stag's horn sumach. They grow at an enormous rate, which is just as well as the plant tends to behave as a herbaceous perennial in our climate, and must start again from scratch each year. The leaves are very decorative, pinnate with four leaflets. They are satisfyingly tropical-looking, being typically vetch-like, but of great size. During the day, the leaves spread themselves open but towards the evening fold up, almost like green butterflies, and droop towards the stem. The emerging leaves are protected by inflated stipules, which are bract-like growths forming small puffy cushions. These are extremely decorative, being pale green streaked with purple, and many people take them for flowers at first glance. In fact, the large soft-yellow pea flowers dangle gracefully from between the leaf axils, but they arrive so late that they only make it if autumn is mild and frost-free. We manage to flower it one year out of two in southern Scotland, and it is well worth the wait.

Amicia zygomeris is ideal for those newly-fashionable tropical borders, which rely upon plants that look exotic, but are reasonably hardy in our climate. It will survive about -10° C (14° F), so it needs a warm spot with a little winter protection. One has flourished for many years at Chelsea Physic Garden in London, and there are reports of them surviving quite low temperatures in gardens all over the country. So look out for it, and if you do see it for sale anywhere, snap it up.

LEFT

GOAT'S RUE *Galega officinalis* 'Alba'

LUPINUS VERSICOLOR

David Douglas, who introduced so many good plants to European gardens in the early eighteenth century, brought us this little lupin from the Pacific coast of America. Spanning virtually the full range of the west coast from British Columbia to California, it lives within sight and sound of the surf, eking out a bracing existence on sandy beaches and dunes. Prostrate stems, 60 cm (2 ft) long, sprawl over the sand, anchored at intervals by fleshy roots. These roots, which are bright yellow, were cooked and eaten by the American Indians who regarded them as a valuable food source.

It is a pretty plant with the usual palmate leaves typical of the genus, but in this case covered with a protective pelt of short silvery hairs lending a delicately frosted effect to the foliage. This protects the plant from salt-laden winds and even regular dousing by seaspray. The flowers are carried in irregular whorls, on spikes 10 cm (4 in) high. Keel and standard are violet-blue, often spotted with black, but the standard shades out to yellow or cream towards the centre, giving it the synonym *Lupinus versicolor*, which means turning colour.

A few nurseries stock plants, or seed is occasionally available through exchanges. Obviously a must for seaside gardens, it is a

BELOW
Amicia zygomeris

pretty tough cookie, and will thrive even away from its Baywatch-type habitat. No drainage can be too sharp, no soil too impoverished. A raised bed or sink which is practically pure grit would suit it perfectly, and a position in as sunny and exposed a spot as your garden can manage. One thing that always puzzles me about this largely American genus is the spelling of it. To us they are 'lupins', but in their native country they are lupines. Is it a dropped 'e', or an imported one? Answers, please, from any passing etymologist.

LOTUS BERTHELOTII

One recent gardening trend that is very welcome is the explosion of interest in container and conservatory gardening. Recent baking summers have reinforced this trend; and garden centres are stocking an ever more adventurous range of tender plants. Bedded out for summer or used in containers, these plants add spice and topspin to the summer garden.

Lotus berthelotii comes from Tenerife, but is probably virtually extinct in the wild. It has a cascading habit of growth and is tailor-made for an exotic hanging basket or, as I prefer it, brimming over the edge of a tall pot. The woody stems are densely clothed with palmate leaves, but these are so numerous, and the individual leaflets so fine, that the stems appear to be surrounded by a soft fuzz of silvery-green foliage. If the plant becomes starved, its foliage is

especially pale, and the froth of silver-green leaves have a look of sea-spume about them.

The flowers, too, have a maritime appearance. They are vivid scarlet, and shaped like the long curved claw of a lobster. The common name is parrot's beak, but the flowers are very like another exotic pea, the wall-shrub *Clianthus puniceus*, familiarly called lobster claw. The keeled flowers of *Lotus berthelotii* are borne in clusters at the ends of the branchlets, so although only 2.5 cm (1 in) long, their profusion makes a great impact. The best clone, Kew form, has very silvered foliage and flowers of pure scarlet.

It will not tolerate any frost, so must be overwintered indoors, and then cut back in spring ready for another season. Better practice, however, is to take cuttings in late summer from unflowered side shoots. They root and overwinter easily; moreover, young plants flower much more generously. And the more you have of this flauntingly beautiful plant, the more pleasure it gives.

INDIGOFERA HETERANTHA

Indigofera heterantha must be a wonderful sight in the wild. It comes from the western end of the Himalayas, Afghanistan, through Himachal Pradesh and western Nepal into Bhutan, forming dense thickets on dry hillsides. A mature specimen is an intricate network of twiggy branches, 3 m (10 ft) tall. The cat's cradle effect of crisscrossed branches predominates even in summer, as the pinnate leaves are so delicate and light that they add virtually no substance to the airy framework. They are, however, entirely typical of the pea family in having 13–21 leaflets emanating from a central midrib, as well as a tendency to fold up at night, a characteristic shared with many shrubby legumes. Its charm lies in the delicacy of form, and the feathery elegance of the foliage.

In early summer the shrub throws out a veil of rosy-mauve flowers, carried in clusters. No dull and lumpy foliage or stolid habit of growth detract from their frothy beauty. Indeed, the whole light concoction of branch, leaf and flower looks like something put together by a pointillist painter, and it holds its own with any of the star performers of the June garden.

The snag is hardiness. Dry gardens seem to have no problem with it, and although sometimes knocked back by frost, it regenerates from the base like a fuchsia. In south-west Scotland we grow many borderline hardy plants, but lost indigofera in no more than an average winter. I suspect conditions were much too damp for it. We shall keep trying, though, because last summer I fell in love with it all over again. At Tintinhull a quartet of indigoferas, marking the intersection of two paths, are pruned into loose spheres. I saw them in full flower above a carpet of low-growing roses, and the result was a perfect piece of garden theatre.

Lupinus versicolor

PARROT'S BEAK
Lotus berthelotii

Indigofera heterantha

THE
LILY
FAMILY

*The lily family has something for every garden
and every gardener. The delicate fritillaries and
erythroniums of spring are followed by a huge
range of stately summer lilies, their bold, elegant
blooms bringing a new dimension to the flower
border. No garden should be without them.*

LILIACEAE

FLOWER FACTS
THE BIRDS AND THE BEES

LILIES AND THEIR relations have captured the hearts of many people over many centuries. The Madonna lily *(Lilium candidum)* was grown by the Egyptians and Cretans as far back as 1750 BC, and the flowers of this family still possess a certain romance.

There is a great deal of discussion about what is in and what is out of the lily family. One grouping only leaves about 20 hard-core members, which are characterized by their large, showy flowers, and leaves attached to the stems. Even with 20 members, there is certainly enough to fill a border of any dimension. The Liliaceae come in all sizes, from 5 cm (2 in) *Gagea peduncularis* to the unbelievable 3 m (10 ft) spires of *Cardiocrinum giganteum*, the giant lily of the Himalayas.

The Liliaceae are a little different to all the other families chosen for this book as they belong to a sub-class called the monocotyledons. As the name suggests, they are characterized by having one cotyledon, or seed leaf, so when you grow them from seed they literally come up like grass. All the other families in this book belong to the dicotyledons, and no prizes for guessing how many seed leaves they pop up with! The true leaves of many Liliaceae are also grass-like, as they have parallel veins rather than the typical branched veins of the dicotyledons.

The members of the lily family, in its largest sense, are essentially herbaceous and have storage organs such as corms, rhizomes or bulbs. The flower parts of this family occur in multiples of three, usually six. The lilies themselves have three sepals and three petals which are almost indistinguishable from each other. The family's flowers are regular, that is symmetrical, and bisexual, containing both male and female parts. They are one of the easiest families in which to study sexual reproduction as in most genera the female part, the stigma, rises up for all to see in the centre of the stamens, surrounded by six attendant stamens. The stigma begins to glisten when it is ready to accept pollen and, when the male parts are ready to shed their pollen, they appear precariously perched on the top of their filaments, like a see-saw, ready to tip the pollen out on to a visiting pollinator. In florist shops these orange and yellow anthers are removed as they just as readily tip their load on to passing visitors and the pollen, once it gets onto your clothes, is tricky to remove.

Lily family members are mainly pollinated by insects attracted by honey secreted by the ovaries or exposed nectaries at the base of the petals. If you look into the blooms of *Fritillaria imperialis* the nectaries shine out, just like enticing, glistening white pearls.

LEFT
Lilium pardilinum

WILD LILIES

ASTUNNING, THOUGH RARE, sight, in spring is the purple haze of a meadow full of snake's head fritillaries *(Fritillaria meleagris)*. In order to appreciate them, you have to get right in there, even lying beneath them, to look up into their nodding cobra-like heads of chequerboard pink and purple petals. The latin name comes from *fritillus*, a dice box, referring to the box-like shape of the flower and *meleagris*, a guinea fowl, relating to the speckled petals. Other names include Turkey-hen flowers, leopard lilies, and chequered lilies. North Meadow at Cricklade in Gloucestershire holds a high proportion of the British population of snake's head fritillaries; about 1,500,000 in 44 hectares (108 acres). The meadow, a site of special scientific interest (SSSI), which floods regularly in the winter, is on the silty soils between the rivers Thames and Churn.

The flowers are there due to a management regime that goes back hundreds of years. A hay crop, grown during the summer, is cut after 1st July and moved off by 12th August. The meadow is then grazed as common land which prevents stronger grass species from taking over. These grazing rights, called Lammas rights, have been granted to local people for 800 years. The animals are removed by 12th February to allow the vegetation to recommence its growth cycle.

The lifecycle of the fritillaries fits in perfectly with the system. The plants flower early in the year and rapidly build up reserves before being overshadowed

BELOW LEFT
SNAKESHEAD FRITILLARIA
Fritillaria meleagris

BELOW RIGHT
LILY OF THE VALLEY
Convalaria majalis

by other meadow species. Their seeds are shed before the hay is cut, and the parent bulbs then lie dormant in the soil between June and August. After the hay is removed, new shoots grow up to just below the surface and then go dormant again as the weather cools down. As soon as spring arrives, they take their chance and grow up rapidly before the meadow grasses get going.

Before 1930, snake's head fritillaries were found in 27 counties; now the plants are confined to nine counties in southern England. But as snake's head fritillaries were not recorded in the wild until 1736, are they native to Britain at all? Some believe them to be escapees from seventeenth-century gardens, while others conclude that they have always been here. In Britain, fritillaries are found around the Thames valley, and on the continent around the Rhine valley. Before the North Sea opened up, these rivers were joined, and the fritillaries may have spread that way. Here, they could grow in the woodlands until they discovered a niche in winter-grazed hay meadows.

Other native members of the hard-core lily family are few and far between. *Gagea lutea,* the yellow star of Bethlehem, flowers even before the fritillaries. It is a delicate little bulbous plant with umbels of yellow flowers that open only at midday. Another rarity, the wild tulip *Tulipa sylvestris,* flowers at the same time as the fritillaries. The drooping buds become more erect as they expand into solitary, star-like yellow flowers. Then comes the Snowdon lily, *Lloydia serotina.* Only 5–15 cm (2–6 in) high, the slender leaves and stem support a solitary white flower, veined with red, which appears in June. It is found in Snowdonia in Wales and also in southern Germany. As a protected species, it must not be picked.

Taxonomists have split several native Liliaceae into other families, including false hellebores (*Veratrum album*), asphodels (*Tofieldia* and *Narthecium*) and a range of alliums, scillas, colchicums, and Solomon's seals *(Polygonatum).* Two fragrant examples are lily-of-the-valley *(Convallaria majalis)* and bluebells *(Hyacinthoides non-scripta),* sometimes placed in the families Convallariaceae and Hyacinthaceae respectively. With its spicy scent and white bell flowers, the beautiful lily-of-the-valley is found throughout Europe, from Britain to the Caucasus. The bluebell, another favourite, has not only swapped families but also changed generic names many times. As well as having fantastic scent and colour, this plant's sap was used as a paper glue and for sticking feathers onto arrows.

But where among the true natives and renamed natives is the lily? *Lilium martagon* crops up in many of the old British and European floras. Found in south-west England, it may be a naturalized garden escapee, having been cultivated since Tudor times. Earlier herbals mention a red lily and, as martagons are sometimes called the Lily of Nazareth, it is possible they were brought back by Crusaders.

RIGHT
BLUEBELL
Hyacinthoides non-scripta

WILD LILIES

RAMSONS
Allium ursinum

WILD ASPARAGUS
Asparargus officinalis

MEADOW SAFFRON
Colchicum autumnale

LILY-OF-THE-VALLEY
Convallaria majalis

SNAKE'S HEAD FRITILLARY
Fritillaria meleagris

YELLOW STAR OF BETHLEHEM
Gagea lutea

BLUEBELL
Hyacinthoides non-scripta

MARTAGON LILY
Lilium martagon

SNOWDON LILY
Lloydia serotina

BOG ASPHODEL
Narthecium ossifragum

COMMON STAR OF BETHLEHEM
Ornithogalum umbellatum

COMMON SOLOMON'S SEAL
Polygonatum multiflorum

BUTCHER'S BROOM
Ruscus aculeatus

AUTUMN SQUILL
Scilla autumnalis

SPRING SQUILL
Scilla verna

SCOTTISH ASPHODEL
Tofieldia pusilla

WILD TULIP
Tulipa sylvestris

FALSE HELLEBORINE
Veratrum album

THE FLOWERING YEAR

ALTHOUGH THE LILY family has shrunk in recent years due to reclassification, within each remaining genus the range is huge. The fritillaries are one of the first members to flower in the spring. The well-known purple snake's head fritillary (*Fritillaria meleagris*) and the taller bright-orange crown imperial *(F. imperialis)* flower in April. Slightly earlier, with the help of a bulb frame comes *F. stenanthera*, its milky-white flowers flushed with pink, and *F. carica*, a beautiful clear yellow. The season can be extended with later flowering species including *F. persica* 'Adiyaman' with purple grape-coloured flowers and *F. uva-vulpis* with plum-coloured blooms edged with gold. Both flower about four weeks after the snake's head and are fairly easy.

Erythroniums are a useful low-growing plant for the garden, especially under deciduous trees. April-flowering species and hybrids include the violet *E. dens-canis*, the yellow *E. grandiflorum*, the pink *E.* 'Joanna' and the creamy-yellow *E.* 'White Beauty'.

Better known are the ubiquitous tulips, which fit into almost any colour scheme in the spring border. Early species get going in February and include *Tulipa kaufmanniana*, creamy-white with red-brushed petals, *T. pulchella humilis*; soft pinkish violet, and the incredible *T. pulchella violacea* which is globular and fuschia-pink. Most of the species come in April in colours ranging from pale apricot (*T. batalinii* 'Apricot Jewel') to red and green *(T. clusiana* 'Cynthia'). In May the late species flower. They include *Tulipa viridiflora*, with twisted colour mixes in the petals, the elegant pointed petals of the lily-flowered tulips, single lates and oddities such as *T.* 'Black Parrot', which is dark purple and frilled.

Spring cannot be left behind without a brief mention of calochortus, a small genus containing some delicate early-flowering bulbs. *Calochortus alba,* the fairy lantern, has stunning white or pink pendent bell-shaped flowers, and *C. luteus* bears three-petalled yellow flowers with central chocolate blotches.

FEBRUARY

WATERLILY TULIP
Tulipa kaufmanniana
February–April

MARCH

TULIP
Tulipa tarda
March

APRIL

AMERICAN TROUT LILY
Erythronium revolutum
April–May

SNAKE'S HEAD FRITILLARY
Fritillaria meleagris
April–May

YELLOW STAR OF BETHLEHEM
Gagea lutea
April–June

TULIP
Tulipa 'Diana'
April

TULIP
Tulipa praecox
April

TULIP
Tulipa 'Queen of Night'
April–May

MAY

YELLOW MARIPOSA
Calochortus luteus
May

FRITILLARY SPECIES
Fritillaria pontica
May–June

TULIP
Tulipa marjolletii
May

JUNE

MADONNA LILY
Lilium candidum
June–July

NOTHOLIRION
Notholirion campanulatum
June

JULY

GIANT HIMALAYAN LILY
Cardiocrinum giganteum
July–August

EASTER LILY
Lilium longiflorum
July–August

TURK'S CAP LILY
Lilium martagon
July

SNOWDON LILY
Lloydia serotina
July

NOMOCHARIS
Nomocharis mairei syn.
N. pardanthina
July–August

AUGUST

**GOLDEN-RAYED LILY
OF JAPAN**
Lilium auratum
August–September

ORIENTAL LILY
Lilium 'Mona Lisa'
August–September

Lilium speciosum
August–September

SEPTEMBER

AUTUMN CROCUS
Colchicum 'Conquest'
September–November

TOAD LILY
Tricyrtis latifolia
September–November

Back to tulips and *Tulipa sprengeri*, the scarlet-red tulip which flowers as late as June and takes us from spring into summer. In June and July come two futher rarities: *Nomocharis mairei*, for example, with its open-spotted flowers, and *Notholirion campanulatum* with funnel-shaped pendent pink bells up the stem. Also in July, the lily as tall as the trees makes its appearance: *Cardiocrinum giganteum*.

The true lilies, *Lilium*, containing a large array of garden hybrids and stunning species, flower from June to September. The main hybrid groups are as follows: the Asiatics flower around June and have upright flowers; the trumpets, with trumpet-shaped flowers (of course!) flower around July and August; the relatively new North hybrids come into their own in midsummer and the orientals, with their sweet, spicy fragrance and long-lasting blooms, flower in August.

As well as the hybrids, there are many stunning lily species. *Lilium candidum,* the white fragrant Madonna lily, flowers in June, followed in July by the spotted, orange *L. pardalinum,* the ivory trumpets of *L. regale* and the turk's cap *L. martagon* types which look beautiful naturalized in a woodland garden. Tiger lilies *(L. tigrinum)* and *L. auratum*, the golden-rayed lily of Japan, bloom in August, and *Lilium speciosum,* with bowl-shaped, fragrant white flowers takes the border into September. A half-hardy species, it is ideal for a pot in a cool greenhouse.

Three black sheep, now placed in families of their own, are tricyrtis, the toad lilies, colchicums, the autumn crocuses and kniphofias, the red-hot pokers, or torch lilies. These take us through to November, as a grand finale.

KEY
All calendar entries are perennial bulbs.

LILY DIRECTORY

TYPE OF PLANT	(H) HEIGHT (S) SPREAD	CONDITIONS REQUIRED (SEE KEY)	PLANT TYPE AND CULTIVATION TIP	PROPAGATION
Cardiocrinum giganteum	**H** 2.5–3 m (8–10 ft) **S** 90 cm (3 ft)	◐☀❉❉	Monocarpic perennial. Feed lot and lots!	Seed or offsets.
Colchicum 'Conquest', *C. alpinum* 'Antares', *C.* 'Prinses Astrid'	**H** 30 cm (1 ft) **S** 30 cm (1 ft)	◐☀◐❉❉❉	Deciduous bulb. Likes woodland conditions.	Division (slow).
ERYTHRONIUM *Erythronium revolutum* Johnsonii group, *E. oregonum, E.* 'Pagoda'	**H** 30 cm (1 ft) **S** 30 cm (1 ft)	◐☀❉❉❉ / ❉❉	Deciduous bulb. Likes woodland conditions.	Division or seed.
FRITILLARIA *Fritillaria imperialis*	**H** 90 cm (3 ft) **S** 30 cm (1 ft)	◐☀❉❉❉	Deciduous bulb. Plant 15 cm (6in) deep on side. Feed with potash in autumn.	Scales or seed.
Fritillaria meleagris	**H** 30 cm (1 ft) **S** 15 cm (6 in)	◐☀❉❉❉	Deciduous bulb. Likes meadow conditions.	Seed, bulb.
Fritillaria messanensis ssp. *gracilis*	**H** 15 cm (6 in) **S** 15 cm (6 in)	◐☀❉❉	Alpine bulb. Sun and grit.	Seed.
Fritillaria orientalis	**H** 30 cm (1 ft) **S** 30 cm (1 ft)	◐☀❉❉	Alpine bulb. As above.	Seed.
Fritillaria verticilliata	**H** 60 cm (2 ft) **S** 30 cm (1 ft)	◐☀❉	Alpine bulb. Gritty soil.	Division or seed.
Kniphofia species	**H** 1.2 m (4 ft) **S** 90 cm (3 ft)	◐☀❉❉❉	Herbaceous perennial Moist soil in summer.	Division or seed in spring.
ASIATIC HYBRIDS *Lilium* 'Milano'	**H** 90 cm (3 ft) **S** 30 cm (1 ft)	◐◐☀◐❉❉❉	Deciduous bulb. Plant healthy bulbs 15 cm (6 in) deep between autumn and spring.	Detach bulblets in late summer, or detach and grow bulb scales in summer or when planting.
Lilium 'Connecticut King'	**H** 90 cm (3 ft) **S** 30 cm (1 ft)	◐◐☀◐❉❉❉	Deciduous bulb. As above.	As above.

LILIUM				
Lilium auratum	H 1.5 m (5 ft) S 45 cm (18 in)	◌◑☼◐✳✳	Deciduous bulb. Plant bulbs 23cm (9in) deep.	Seed, scales, bulblets.
Lilium bulbiferum	H 75 cm (30 in) S 45 cm (18 in)	◌◑☼◐✳✳✳	Deciduous bulb. Plant bulbs 15cm (6in) deep.	Seed, bulbils, bulblets or scales.
Lilium candidum	H 90 cm (3 ft) S 90 cm (3 ft)	◌◑☼✳✳✳	Deciduous bulb. Prefers limy soil.	Seed and scales.
Lilium nepalense	H 60 cm (2 ft) S 1.8 m (6 ft)	◑☼✳✳	Deciduous bulb. Tends to runner underground.	Seed and scales.
Lilium regale	H 60–1.8 m (2–6 ft) S 60 cm (2 ft)	◑☼✳✳	Deciduous bulb. Plant 17 cm (7 in) deep from autumn to spring.	Seed, scales or bulblets.
NORTH HYBRIDS				
Lilium x marhan	H 1.5-1.8 m (5-6 ft) S 30 cm (1 ft)	◌◑◐✳✳✳	Deciduous bulb. Plant 15–20 cm (6–8in) deep between autumn and spring.	Scales, bulblets.
Lilium 'Marie North', L. 'Peggy North'	H 90-1.2 m (3-4 ft) S 45 cm (18 in)	◌◑☼◐✳✳✳	Deciduous bulb Plant 15cm (6in) deep from autumn to spring.	Scales, bulbils or bulblets.
Lilium martagon	H 1.5 m (5 ft) S 30 cm (1ft)	◌◑☼◐✳✳✳	Deciduous bulb Mulch in spring.	Seed, scales, bulblets.
Lilium sanguineum purpureum	H 1.5 m (5 ft) S 30 cm (1 ft)	◌◑☼◐✳✳✳	Deciduous bulb plant bulbs 15-20 cm (6-8 in) deep.	Scale, bulblets.
ORIENTAL HYBRID LILIES				
Nomocharis mairei	H 90 cm (3 ft) S 30 cm (1 ft)	◑◐✳✳✳	Deciduous bulb. Do not disturb bulbs. Peat bed.	Fresh seed.
Tricyrtis latifolia	H 90 cm (3 ft)	◑☼◐✳✳✳	Rhizomatous perennial Needs humus rich soil.	Division and seed.
TULIPA				
Tulipa 'Fancy Frills' Tulipa 'Jacqueline', Tulipa 'Menton'	H 75 cm (30 in) S 23 cm (9 in)	◌☼✳✳✳	Deciduous bulb. Lift when foliage has died and store dry during summer.	Remove small bulbs from around base and grow on.
Tulipa 'Lord Fredrick Cavendish'	H 60 cm (2 ft) S 23 cm (9 in)	◌☼◐✳✳	Deciduous bulb As above.	As above.

KEY

◌ Well drained soil   ◑ Moist soil   ● Wet soil   ☼ Sun   ◐ Partial shade   ✦ Tolerates full shade
✳ Half-hardy to 0°C (32°F)   ✳✳ Frost-hardy to -5°C (23°F)   ✳✳✳ Fully hardy to -15°C (5°F)

THE GARDENS

LILIES IN A SCOTTISH GARDEN

For years, Dr Peter Waister's interest in lilies was restricted to a small clump of L. regale. *Then, in 1987, he took on the propagation of a unique group of cultivars bred by Chris North, an ex-colleague from the Scottish Crop Research Institute (SCRI). The cooler Scottish climate suits these and the other lilies he grows.*

MATURE TREES AND shrubs and a peaceful location combine to make Peter's a secret garden. Meandering paths open into small glades of lawn beneath trees creating light shade. Although it was the North hybrids I had come to see, we first looked at other lilies to identify some of the nine divisions that make up the genus. They all looked very much at home in pools of light between other plants.

Much loved by florists are the Asiatic hybrids, with characteristic upward-looking, scentless blooms on stems some 90 cm (3 ft) high. Peter had chosen warm, spicy colours like coppery-red 'Milano' and yellow 'Connecticut King'. 'These were planted six years ago and have made bright strong clumps,' commented Peter.

Due to Scottish weather, Peter has to grow the golden-rayed lily of Japan *(L. auratum)* in pots under cover. One of the most spectacular lilies in cultivation, this oriental species bears 12–30 flowers on stems capable of reaching up to 1.5 m (5 ft) tall. Each bloom can reach as much as to 30 cm (1 ft) across and look right at

LEFT
Lilium 'Milano'

RIGHT
THE GOLDEN-RAYED LILY OF JAPAN
Lilum auratum

you, emitting a sweet, almost overpowering perfume. 'Used as a parent with *L. speciosum*, this lily has produced the shorter, pink-flowered hybrid 'Mona Lisa',' said Peter. The blooms of oriental hybrids are usually scented and can be bowl- or trumpet-shaped, flat or recurved (turk's cap-shaped). An elegant group, they tend to flower a little later than the Asiatics.

L. regale is one of several species from which the trumpet lilies are derived. 'This originates from a 50-mile stretch in a Chinese valley,' said Peter. 'Yet despite its specific location, is widely grown, thriving in moist, well-drained soils. Unlike most other lilies, it tolerates, if not actually prefers, mildly alkaline conditions.' Plants 60 cm–1.8 m (2–6 ft) tall produce up to 25 fragrant, trumpet-shaped blooms 12–15 cm (5–6 in) long. Basically white, they have purple-pink stripes on the outside and are flushed with yellow within.

The most notable lilies in Peter's garden are what I shall refer to as the 'North Hybrids', though strictly speaking, they belong under the umbrella of pendent-flowered Asiatics. In 1966, Chris North embarked on a breeding programme at SCRI to develop lilies ideal for British growing conditions. 'Chris identified the parent lilies he wanted to use, including *L. lankongense*, but the seed from the crosses he made turned out to be sterile,' said Peter. 'The embryos were alive, so he grew them on in test tubes, using what was then a new technique.'

ABOVE LEFT
Lilium 'Mona Lisa'

ABOVE RIGHT
Lilium 'Connecticut King'

RIGHT
Lilium 'Marie North'

FAR RIGHT
Lilium 'Peggy North'

140

The end results were strong lilies with good flower colours and a structure similar to turk's cap varieties. They also appear resistant to the virus infections which can plague lilies, weakening and distorting their growth.

The first five hybrids North selected were named after Greek deities, then he named a further ten after female members of his family. Of these, pale peach-pink 'Rosemary North', delicate pink 'Barbara North', and red 'Karen North' have been given the RHS Award of Garden Merit, an accolade not bestowed lightly. The next challenge was to bring the plants into cultivation. Peter was due to retire from his post as head of Crop Sciences. 'I cannot recall the exact sequence of events,' he says, 'but Chris must have talked me into taking them on.'

Using a specially adapted greenhouse, Peter concentrates on propagating and maintaining virus-free plants. He works with nurseryman Bruce Robertson, who is building up good stocks of North lilies, and bringing them to a wider audience.

Surprisingly few gardeners seem able to establish good clumps of lilies. 'Look carefully at what you are buying,' said Peter. 'Bulbs are lifted during autumn, the ideal time to plant, but most are stored and sold in spring.' The quality of storage can affect performance. Neither the scales nor perennial roots below the bulb must dry out, otherwise all the energy goes into replacing roots instead of flowering.

To avoid virus infection, grow lilies between other plants, so aphids can clean their mouthparts of any infected lily sap. Never grow tulips and lilies together.

'If lilies have a reputation for difficulty, it is probably because of bulb quality,' said Peter. 'Wild species grow in a huge range of habitats, from sandy soils to peats, in wet and dry areas, and in extremes of cold and warm. So there is probably a lily for every garden, given a supply of good stock.'

LILY PROPAGATION

Most lilies look their best when planted in generous groups between other plants. To achieve this, a gardener either needs a large budget, or a sound knowledge of propagation. Nurseryman Bruce Robertson talked Anne Swithinbank through the various methods used. Timing, technical skills and aftercare are all important.

AFTER FLOWERING, MOST lilies set seed, which can be collected when the pods are brown and dry. 'Put the flat seeds into see-through envelopes, then hold them up to the light,' said Bruce. 'The line in the middle of the seed is the embryo and if that is in place, there is a good chance of germination.'

To sow, prepare a 17-20 cm (7-8 in) pot by filling with seed compost to which 20 per cent extra grit has been added to ensure good drainage. 'Sow the seed fresh, soon after it has been collected,' advised Bruce, 'space it out flat on the compost before covering with a thin layer of grit, then place in a shaded greenhouse or cold frame to shield the seedlings from hot sun. Germination will be variable, but expect flowering plants within four years.' This is an excellent method for species like *L. regale*, but will give variable results from hybrid parents.

Another simple method is using the stem bulbils produced by lilies like *L. bulbiferum* and *L. lancifolium* (formerly *L. tigrinum*). Miniature bulbs appear just above the leaves where they join the stem. 'The logical time to collect bulbils is

LEFT
Lilium bulbiferum
hybrid

RIGHT
REGAL LILY
Lilum regale

FAR RIGHT
**LILY SCALES
WITH BULBILS**

when the stem is dying back in late summer,' said Bruce. Set them 2.5 cm (1 in) apart in boxes or pots of free-draining compost. Cover lightly with grit and stand in a cold greenhouse or coldframe. Plant out the following autumn.

Some lilies, *L. longiflorum* and the North hybrids, for instance, also produce bulbils just above the bulb. When mature bulbs go dormant in autumn, they can be lifted, and the bulbils removed. Bruce plants his large and small bulbs back into the well-drained soil, covered by twice their depth of soil.

Scaling is a specialist method where some of the healthy, swollen modified leaves which make up the bulb are pulled off and encouraged to grow new bulbils. 'I would suggest the parent lily is lifted in bloom,' said Bruce. 'This way you can be absolutely sure you are propagating the desired lily. A few scales can be removed from new lily bulbs just before planting.'

The plump scales are washed in cold water, dipped in a solution of fungicide, then placed in a polythene bag containing about four times their volume of damp vermiculite. Leave this in a warm place at 21° C (70° F) until the scales sprout small bulbs, complete with roots – about three months. After this, the scales can be removed and potted separately. Plant one per 8 cm (3 in) pot, or dibble several into a deep tray, so the tips are just protruding.

Keep frost-free until leaves grow in spring, then gradually harden off during summer, so that in autumn, the developing bulbils can be lifted, separated and planted to mature as individuals in pots or trays. 'Depending on type, they can reach flowering size in as little as two years,' said Bruce.

THE MARTAGON LILY GARDEN

Martagon lilies are well known for their tall stems of distinctive, turk's cap flowers. Their genteel beauty is best appreciated in a woodland setting, like that of Quarry Wood, near Newbury in Berkshire. This garden was legendary in lily circles even before Dee Martyn Simmons and her husband bought it in 1953.

WALTER BENTLEY VMH chose Quarry Hill because its acid soil would suit the plants he wanted to grow. He died having turned 3.5 hectares (9 acres) of scrub into a garden renowned for its collection of lilies. Soon after his death, the property was sold, the existing head gardener died and there were no written records to help the new owners.

Dee recalls her feelings soon after moving into her new home. 'We had no idea that our garden was famous,' she said. 'After one disastrous attempt to find a new head gardener, I decided to tackle it myself and began to feel my way around, mostly by weeding through the plants on my hands and knees.' After six years she had the good fortune to employ Maurice Woodgates, who became equally devoted to the garden, and although retired, still loves and works among the plants.

Dee discovered that many of Walter Bentley's original plantings remained. Orange-flowered *L. henryi* and *L. hansonii*, red-flowered *L. canadense rubrum,* and of course, many different forms of *L. martagon* were growing and seeding between

LEFT
Lilium martagon

RIGHT
Lilium x *marhan*

FAR RIGHT
Lilium sanguineum
purpureum

exotic trees and shrubs. 'I feel very privileged,' she says, 'because through the garden, I became accepted as part of the horticultural world.' She is a member and past Chairman of the RHS Lily Group, as well as part of the committee responsible for judging the main exhibits at the Chelsea Flower Show.

Turk's cap lilies manage to be both exotic and colourful, yet subtly dainty. On my midsummer visit, a group of *L.* x *marhan* looked entirely at home in their setting, with red-spotted, orange flowers nodding from stems reaching 1.5–1.8 m (5–6 ft) tall. Another bend in the border revealed a group of unusual, dark red *L. sanguineum purpureum*.

The lilies seed where they will, and sprouting precariously out of the midst of a hydrangea was an exquisite pink bloom. 'We called this martagon seedling 'Mildred's Pearl' after my late sister,' said Dee. Seed is also collected, germinated and the young lilies planted out or distributed, in some cases, around the world. 'Our plants thrive on common sense and plenty of organic matter,' said Dee.

Dee's favourite was lemon-yellow *L. monadelphum*. Not the easiest to grow, it resents disturbance and can take several years to settle down. Maurice loves *L. pyrenaicum,* the greenish yellow-flowered turk's cap lily of the Pyrenees. 'It grows wild in Devon hedgerows,' he said, 'and I can remember admiring it as a child.' There is no doubt in Dee's mind that the influence of one who builds and loves a garden lives on. 'I wish Walter Bentley could look back on his garden, and feel the pleasure it has given to us and gardeners from all over the world.'

ENGLISH TULIPS

Among the most widely grown plants in the lily family, tulips have a fascinating history. In seventeenth-century Holland, they caused 'tulip mania' when bulbs bearing attractively marked (or 'broken') flowers were traded for vast sums. Today, the Wakefield Tulip Society aims to conserve these unusual plants.

IRONICALLY, THE ONCE-coveted 'broken' tulips are no longer grown in Holland because their unusual markings are the result of virus infection. The mass production of tulips is such big business that the last thing the Dutch need are old varieties which might infect their crops. However, they live on in England, where few tulips are grown commercially and strict quarantine rules do not apply, and are now called 'English Tulips'. Despite this, they nearly died out this century, which is why the work of the Wakefield Tulip Society is so important.

Originally a keen grower and exhibitor of daffodils, society Secretary Wendy Akers married into a tulip family. 'My father-in-law was a great tulip grower and breeder, and my husband caught the bug from him. Even so, after 30 years he only managed to create two new varieties.' Wendy's son-in-law is keen, but must start his breeding programme while young enough to stand a chance of success.

'You start with a breeder bulb,' explained Wendy, 'itself the result of controlled pollination. Flowering takes seven years from seed, and only then can it be assessed

LEFT
DUTCH TULIPS

RIGHT
Tulipa 'Lord Frederick Cavendish'

for quality. The breeder bulbs have to be bulked up and grown in large numbers. Only one in a thousand will break into a colourful variety worth keeping and naming. Bad breaks are pulled up and, historically, ground underfoot!'

Healthy tulip flowers have two layers of cells; in a 'broken' flower, these separate into a base colour and markings. 'The virus doesn't kill the tulip, though it can spoil ordinary varieties and will kill lilies,' said Wendy.

Once a bulb has 'broken', it remains true, with young bulblets retaining the same markings. These are described as feathers or flames. A 'feather' has a clear-coloured base, with markings around the edge, like 'James Wild' which has reddish brown marks on yellow. 'Flame' markings are found in varieities such as 'Lord Frederick Cavendish' and 'Sir Joseph Paxton', where markings run right down into the base.

'Four hundred years ago the only flowers most people had seen were natives, such as bluebells and the like. So you can imagaine that these flamboyant tulips caused great excitement and ladies used to pin the blooms to their dresses.' To begin with, only the very wealthy would have owned them. Plants then spread around, and individual growers joined up to form societies, who grew, admired and exhibited the plants. The Wakefield and North of England Society dates from 1836 and has 230 members. 'Some of the bulbs we own have been handed down from generation to generation,' said Wendy. 'Joining the society and obtaining bulbs from other members is the only way of acquiring them: there are only 25 old varieties of English tulips left.'

Both Wendy and her daughter Sarah grow Dutch tulips as well, which, to keep them virus-free, must be grown in separate gardens or allotments. We took a short drive to Sarah's garden, where she grows a selection of different varieties in rows.

LEFT
Tulipa 'Jacqueline'

RIGHT
Tulipa 'Menton'

FAR RIGHT
Tulipa 'Fancy Frills'

I was amazed to see them still fresh and blooming in June. 'Wakefield is a cool pocket of England and we tend to grow the later-flowered varieties, so they can be shown at the same time as the English tulips,' explained Wendy.

They were sturdy, healthy plants, and had produced large, first-class flowers. Most were some 75 cm (30 in) tall. They were so good, I immediately vowed to try harder with tulips myself. I usually just slot groups between other plants without paying much attention to the soil. I leave mine in from year to year and, though bulbs usually flower again, the quality is not always good.

'We plant in November,' said Wendy, 'setting the bulbs 15 cm (6 in) deep into manured soil. If we were leaving them in, we would plant deeper. In their native Turkey, they receive spring water from the mountains for only a short period and have to complete their growth relatively quickly. By the time the flowers have opened, a new bulb for next year and bulblets are in place too.'

After flowering, plants are dead headed and allowed to die back naturally. They are then lifted, dried, cleaned up and stored in paper bags. 'My favourite job is cleaning and sorting,' said Wendy. 'It is like my harvest. People buy bulbs thinking that they are the best they will ever get. In fact, you can grow even bigger bulbs in subsequent years. I remove bits of old tunic and grade them.' Offsets (young bulbs) are removed and grown on or given away. 'We use the same treatment for English tulips, but without rich soil: their colours are better where the soil is poorer.'

We admired the classic, single-flowered pink 'Menton', fringed cream 'Maja' and dark, brooding purple-black 'Queen of Night'. 'It's a shame bulb flowers are sold in bud,' said Wendy. 'They use all their energy to open, so don't stay fresh for long. Cut tulips when in flower, and they will last from two to four weeks in a cool room.'

PLANTSMAN'S CHOICE

BILL CHUDZIAK

FRITILLARIES

Fritillaries are the sophisticates of the spring garden. Most spring bulbs have a sort of innocent freshness about them; they come in a cheering range of simple colours, sky-blue, jonquil-yellow, creamy white. Fritillaries, on the other hand, have a worldly fascination reflected in their decidedly off-beat colour schemes. The familiar and incomparable crown imperial – *Fritillaria imperialis* – may flaunt its strident orange or yellow flowers, but subtlety is the byword where most fritillaries are concerned. The bell-shaped flowers, elongated or plump according to variety, come in a thrilling palette ranging from deadly-nightshade purple and bitter chocolate through grey-mauves to pallid citron and greeny whites. Several are black with a sloe-like bloom, and many are tessellated, striped, or zoned with distinctly daring colour contrasts.

Some find the tomcat aroma of crown imperials hard to take, but I relish it as the first whiff of spring. It is almost at its strongest when the growing-tip, still invisible, just dislodges the soil-crust. But what about those that have a strong spermatic scent, designed to lure their pollinators, queen wasps and blowflies? Repellent? Well, possibly. But although the charm is often reptilian, it is undoubtedly there. Fritillaries, in short, have glamour.

LEFT

CROWN IMPERIAL *Fritillaria imperialis*

Many are the province of the alpine specialist, to be grown in pans in a controlled environment where they can be guaranteed their summer baking. But there are good garden plants in their ranks. At Craigieburn we love to grow *Fritillaria imperialis* in tubs as spring bedding. They can then be retired to the border where an autumn feed of potash gets them flowering again. Our cool peaty conditions suit *Fritillaria verticillata*. Its hooked leaf tips enable it to hoist itself over neighbouring plants where it sprawls languidly. Immensely elegant, the flowers are coolly chequered green and cream. *Fritillaria pyrenaica* likes similar conditions and has yellow flowers heavily stippled with chocolate.

For a pocket of good soil in a well-drained rock-garden try *Fritillaria acmopetala,* tall and slender, with an inner petticoat of brown-suffused petals and an overskirt of green and white. It is utterly beautiful, but strong-smelling. *Fritillaria michailovskyi* turns up in garden centres occasionally, and is an obliging little character. It has tubby bells the colour of spread Marmite, with a wide butter-yellow frill round the rim. Both these fritillaries do very well in troughs, and this seems a successful way to grow many of the genus. Fanatics might enjoy the challenge of *F. messanensis* or *F. orientalis*. Without going to the lengths of the real enthusiast, the gardener can do a moderate amount of manipulation of both environment and growing medium. In short, have a go. Try any you can get your hands on. They are a surefire way of giving the spring garden real top spin.

Fritillaria messanensis spp. *gracilis*

Fritillaria verticillata

Fritillaria orientalis

Erythronium oregonum

Erythronium 'Pagoda'

MADONNA LILY
Lilium candidum

ERYTHRONIUMS

From the great native woodlands of North America come plants of cool and crystalline beauty. The richness of the spring flora from this region is mouth-watering: trillium, dodecatheon, jeffersonia, sanguinaria, erythronium, a roll-call of desirables shining like the Holy Grail to any gardener with a patch of woodland. Of these plants, the only one which is readily available to the non-specialist is the erythronium. When David Douglas, the great plant-hunter, first came across erythroniums in bud, he mistook them for fritillaries, and there is a distinct family resemblance.

Erythroniums are scrumptious from the moment their noses poke through the soil. Bomb-shaped buds cannon upwards unfurling broad flounces of juicy leaf. In some species, notably the European *Erythronium dens-canis*, these leaves are mottled with brown and olive: one common name is the trout lily, and they do resemble brown trout gliding through sun dappled shallows. Even those whose leaves are predominantly green, like *Erythronium grandiflorum* have, on close inspection, faint cream marbling along the leaf veins, and they are subtly suffused with bronze. This copious foliage is so replete with moisture that it actually feels clammy, and squeaks if rubbed against itself. The erythronium flowers are pure lily. The nodding buds open firstly to a six-petalled star, and then reflex into a classic turk's cap lily shape. They are wonderfully elegant, rather like the upswept roofs of Chinese pagodas. There is a prominent central cluster of stigma and stamens, loaded, in typical lily fashion, with vast amounts of pollen, so abundant that it often spills onto the petals.

Apart from the pink *Erythronium dens-canis* which has been well-known in cultivation for several hundred years, there are two others which are readily available. *Erythronium oregonum* has bronzy marbled leaves and cream flowers with a yellow eye outlined with zigzags of orange. A selection, or possibly a hybrid, of this species is 'White Beauty', and this is a good garden plant, easy, and quick to increase. *Erythronium tuolumnense* has glistening green leaves and rich yellow flowers. A named form is available, 'Pagoda', and this, too, is reliable and easy to grow.

Other erythronium species can be successfully raised from seed obtainable from reliable seed merchants. Fresh seed and exposure to a cold winter gives the best germination. A thin layer of grit on top of the seedpan ensures that the compost stays cool and uniformly moist. Plants should be flowering in your garden within three to five years. Position them in semi-shade in a moist peaty soil enriched with well-rotted leaf mould. It is also worth remembering that they will not tolerate waterlogging but hate to dry out, so a retentive growing medium is the answer. Mimic, in fact, conditions of their native woodland habitat, and they will reward you with their brief but glorious fanfare every spring.

LILIUM CANDIDUM

The history of Europe is embodied in this single flower. *Lilium candidum* is depicted in the wall-paintings of Minoan Crete. It followed the Roman legions as they pushed their empire outward, and the Moors as they expanded into Spain and Portugal. The legionnaires cultivated it for food, and monastic orders adopted it for medicinal use. The Venerable Bede hijacked it from several Roman goddesses and gave it an aura of sanctity as the emblem of the Virgin Mary: white petals for physical purity, gold anthers for spiritual refulgence. In medieval literature it was a stock metaphor for unblemished, if somewhat chilly, chastity. 'Emelye', writes Chaucer of the heroine of 'The Knight's Tale', 'that fairer was to sene/Than is the lilye on his stalke grene'. It also decorated the banners of the Most Christian Kings of France and stylized into the fleur-de-lys, it is still to France what the rose is to England. But only in the nineteenth century was it named Madonna lily, to distinguish it from other white lilies newly introduced from the Far East.

Lilium candidum comes from western Asia and is now rare in the wild. The cultivated form is distinct, broader of petal, larger and more ornamental than wild stock. It is a lovely thing with its pure milk-white petals, glossy leaves, and bright gold stamens. Something of an inverted snob, it often flourishes in cottage gardens, and sulks in grander settings. This could have everything to do with its cultural needs. Being shallow-growing, it dislikes disturbance, and the *laisser faire* approach of cottage gardeners suited it well. It is also susceptible to virus diseases, and in grander gardens became vulnerable to cross-infection from other lilies. Plant it close to the surface in good well-drained loam. Then emulate the cottagers, by refraining from officious horticultural fussing, and simply enjoy its historic beauty.

CARDIOCRINUM GIGANTEUM

For lucky gardeners with cool woodland soil and shelter, *Cardiocrinum giganteum*, the giant Himalayan lily, is one of the most magnificent plants in cultivation.

It takes up to seven years to flower from seed, producing an annually increasing rosette of leaves, which are heart-shaped and slickly glossy as if newly varnished. They are extremely beautiful, but loved by slugs, so encircle them with a *cordon sanitaire* of grit.

The flowering is an event of high drama. In spring, a great hollow stem, 8 cm (3 in) across, emerges from the base. It climbs with Jack-and-the-beanstalk relentlessness to 2.5–3 m (8–10 ft), terminating in a cluster of large flower buds.

RIGHT

GIANT HIMALAYAN LILY *Cardiocrinum giganteum*

Alternately-placed leaves, shining and heart-shaped, diminish in size as they ascend the stem. Finally, in midsummer, the climax arrives and the enormous flowers, up to 20 on each stem, begin to open. They are huge flared trumpets, candlewax-white, green-tinted on the reverse, and flushed with claret at the throat.

As the flowers fade, excellent seed heads, resembling polished green figs, take over. They remain decorative, fading to pale biscuit as summer progresses. Now the main plant dies, leaving behind small offsets, to flower four years later.

Gertrude Jekyll describes the process of growing cardiocrinum on her Surrey sand, involving vast pits, and donkey-loads of compost. Certainly, it needs rich fuel to produce such a high-octane performance, so the rule is: organic matter, and lots of it.

Finally, lest you feel I have over-enthused, this story cuts cardiocrinum down to size. Lady Rosse describes showing a fastidious and acidulous plantsman round the great garden at Nymans. To her puzzlement, he resolutely refused to notice the great lilies of which her father was so proud.

'Won't you admire our giganteum lilies?' said I. 'No, I cannot bear to look at them,' he answered, 'they are like very beautiful women, utterly ruined by thick ankles.'

NOMOCHARIS

The lily family has more than its fair share of ravishing beauties, and the nomocharis are a race of plants of surpassing loveliness, outstanding even in this glamorous family. The almost flat flowers, of delicate translucent pink, are poised butterfly-like on slender wiry stems 90 cm (3 ft) high. In *Nomocharis pardanthina* and its sub-species *Nomocharis farreri*, the flowers are further enhanced by a dusting of claret-coloured freckles. In *Nomocharis mairei*, the spotting extends over the entire flower.

They come from the Himalayas, Tibet through to Burma and western China, and like so many plants from this area, they flourish in northern parts of Britain, where the air is cool and the soil peaty. They are seldom seen in the south, and when they flower – in early summer here in southern Scotland – we are struck by the number of knowledgeable plant-lovers who do not know them. Needless to say, they are invariably entranced by them.

We raise all our nomocharis from seed, a fairly straightforward business. The trick is to get hold of the freshest possible seed (seed exchanges are a good source), and sow it immediately in a roomy seed tray. We swear by fish boxes from the local chip shop. Seedlings germinate like cress, but will perish if pricked out as root disturbance is anathema. Start liquid feeding at six months, and when they have flowered – after about three years – plant them out in handfuls. They seem to have a limitless capacity for hybridization,

however, and few or none of our plants are true to type. We have an array of beautiful mongrels, and the first flowering of a batch of seedlings is always exciting and unpredictable. Some are touched with the merest hint of colour, others strongly suffused with pink and most are speckled, stippled or spotted. All of them are exquisitely beautiful.

LILIUM NEPALENSE

I was just leaving Tinjuri Phedi on the Kanchenjunga range in the Himalayas when I came across *Lilium nepalense* growing wild on a vertical turf bank. To see a colony of this superlative lily was one of the most privileged moments of my life, particularly, as in the wild, it is a shy flowerer. On a subsequent trip to eastern Nepal, we found several patches of foliage, but not a single flower.

The flowers are superb, outstanding even among this most beautiful of flower families. They also have a slightly sinister aura which adds piquancy to their beauty. Great flaring funnels of flowers swept back like the temple roofs of Khatmandu are barely supported by spindly stems. Each 12 cm (5 in) bloom is thick and waxy in texture, varying in colour from tallowy white through greenish ivory to a glimmering pistachio-green. The bottom half of the petals, towards the centre, are stained darkest oxblood, deepening to black towards the nectaries, and shading out to claret towards the mouth of the flower. It is a wickedly sophisticated colour combination, surprising, but also entirely appropriate for the heavy, exotic flowers, drooping languidly on their weak stems.

I saw *Lilium nepalense* at around 3,050 m (10,000 ft), and plants from that altitude are usually borderline hardy in British gardens. It has an odd habit of growth for a lily, producing long underground shoots which ramble several feet from the parent bulb, especially in the loose gritty leaf litter it prefers. A cool greenhouse border would suit it perfectly, or a sheltered spot outside with the very sharpest drainage. It hates winter wet. We grow it in large pots, and it stops visitors in their tracks. But for sheer intensity of experience, nothing beats my first sighting of this extraordinary lily, flowering among turf and meconopsis rosettes in its native Himalayas.

TRICYRTIS

The tricyrtis species, toad lilies, are the quiet beauties of the autumn garden. These herbaceous members of the lily family lack punch when viewed from afar, but cultivate an intimate relationship and you will be beguiled by their reptilian charm. Most are heavily spotted, but there is nothing toad-like about them. The waxy petals,

mostly pink-mottled claret, are more evocative of an exotic lizard or salamander, while the trifurcate (three-forked) stigma, also heavily spotted, is like a trio of darting snake tongues, each forked and curled, but joined at the base.

They come from the eastern Himalayas, Korea, the Philippines, and Japan, where they colonize the fringes of damp woodland. These were precisely the conditions in which I met the exquisite *Tricyrtis bimaculata,* one of the most thrilling plant encounters of a botanical expedition to east Nepal. It is particularly beautiful, with large pale flowers spotted clear pink, but it is rare in cultivation, and, at 3,050 m (10,000 ft), probably borderline hardy. More reliable and available is *Tricyrtis formosanum.* Shiny dark green leaves clothe wiry swaying stems topped by mottled flowers. A stoloniferous plant, it increases well in the woodland loam it prefers. *Tricyrtis macropoda* is similar, as is *Tricyrtis hirta,* which has a white form called 'White Towers'. *Tricyrtis latifolia,* readily available, has a wide ribbed leaf and greeny-yellow flowers. *Tricyrtis ohsumiensis* is a choice dwarf, 22 cm (9 in) tall, with disproportionally large yellow flowers, spotted with brown like a ripe banana. It burns in full sun, so find a cool shady spot.

BELOW
Lilium nepalense

Although tricyrtis with their fibrous root systems seem untypical Liliaceae members, recent experiments in propagation expose family traits. Cuttings taken from the entire length of a flowering stem, each with a section of stem and a single leaf, resulted in the production of a bulbil-like bud, and this effective new technique should increase the availability of this lovely and intriguing genus.

KNIPHOFIAS

Some gardeners revile kniphofias – red-hot pokers – for their stiff and upright habit and shrieking orange colouring. This judgement dates from a time when virtually the only poker generally available was the vibrant *Kniphofia uvaria,* a splendid but unsubtle dazzler for the autumn border. But recent hybridization, and a more general availability of some rare old varieties, have caused many gardeners to look again at this impressive genus.

Virtually all the kniphofias come from South Africa, so hardiness is always under scrutiny. We have lost some varieties in chilly wet winters, but others seem to sail through unscathed, and these, inevitably, have become favourites. 'Yellowhammer', a large-flowered citrus yellow about 90 cm (3 ft) tall, was raised in Ireland at the Slieve Donard nursery. It was untouched by the horrible cold winter of 1995–6, and flowered brilliantly the following August.

'Maid of Orleans' is a pale waxy ivory, a scarce colour in the late summer garden. Sadly, its neat foot-high offspring 'Little Maid' invariably rots off in our wet winters. One of the best 'doers' at Craigieburn is the splendidly named 'Toffee-nosed'. This is a fairly new cultivar from Norfolk, and its pale sulphur yellow flowers turn to burnt umber as they age. It flowers abundantly and late, so is one of the joys of early autumn here. Slightly earlier is the indestructible species *Kniphofia caulescens*. Its elephant trunk stems wander along the ground producing rosettes of architectural grey-green foliage, and the flowers are tangerine fading to chartreuse. So start experimenting with the myriad of marvellous kniphofias, which range from near white, through jade-green, melony pinks and corals, to sunset shades and shocking oranges of the good old-fashioned varieties.

COLCHICUM

One of the best conjuring tricks in the garden is the virtual overnight appearance of colchicum flowers. The naked buds appear like mushrooms from bare earth in autumn, and in a matter of days have opened into large rosy-pink chalices. They closely resemble outsized crocuses, but the leaves, which do not appear until the spring, are the giveaway. They are dark green, broadly strap-shaped, and in need of much elbow room. So plant your colchicums somewhere where the abundant leafage can function as effective and handsome ground cover.

They come from Greece, the Aegean and Turkey, prime bulb country, but there is a rare British native, colloquially known as meadow saffron, or naked ladies *(Colchium autumnale)*. Their predominantly eastern Mediterranean origins are a clue to their cultivation. Give them extra drainage, and try to position them in sun – the flowers close-up in overcast conditions. Most are easy and undemanding, however, and will even flower if the bulbs are left unplanted, an awful thing to do.

Colchicums used to be in the lily family, but taxonomists have had a tidy-up, and they have been promoted to their own family, the Colchicaceae. Ants are the main disseminators, attracted by the sticky goo which coats the seeds. The plant also produces a chemical, colchicine, which is sometimes used in plant breeding, as it stimulates plants into producing double-chromosome, or diploid forms. It is a virulent gastro-intestinal poison, although formerly used as an effective, if risky, treatment for gout.

There are many beautiful species and cultivars, and any that you see for sale are worth growing. 'Waterlily' is a good double, 'The Giant' a reliable all-rounder, white *C. speciosum* 'Album' is a rare and lovely white. But always make sure that you buy only from a reputable source in order to avoid bulbs that have been pillaged from the wild.

TOAD LILY
Tricyrtis latifolia

NAKED LADY
Colchicum 'Conquest'

NAKED LADY
Colchicum alpinum 'Antares'

THE
POPPY
FAMILY

Paint your garden with poppies. Take dazzling orange eschscholzias and piercing blue meconopsis, rich scarlet cornfield poppies or smoky mauve opium poppies and create all the colours of the rainbow. With their vibrant hues and tissue-like petals, this is a family few can resist.

PAPAVERACEAE

FLOWER FACTS
THE BIRDS AND THE BEES

❦

Poppies and their relations can usually be recognized by their beautiful, conspicuous but delicate flowers. Members of the family are found mainly in the temperate zone and in the northern hemisphere, and consist mainly of perennials and annuals with a few shrubs. Botanically it is a pretty straightforward family to identify. In most species, the two sepals that protect the flower bud split open like an egg and fall away to expose the crumpled petals beneath. Like butterflies that have just emerged from a chrysalis, the flowers gently open out, generally revealing four tissue-paper-like petals. As the petals are ironed out by the sun, they reveal whorls of pollen-laden stamens – the pollen varying from yellow to black, depending on the genus. In this bisexual flower, the stamens form a ring around the large female organ which, after fertilization, develops into a capsule full of seeds. Many of you will be familiar with these pepperpot seed capsules, and it is difficult to resist pulling them off and shaking the seeds into the welcoming soil.

One member, glaucium, has seed pods that are very different to those of the rest of the family. They are slim, cylindrical, and very, very long: up to 30 cm (1 ft) in length. Many members of the family, including glaucium, have very oily seeds which are used for a variety of purposes, including making soap.

As usual, the family does have a few uncharacteristic relations. Macleaya, a stunning plant with majestic foliage, does not possess the typical showy petals and its tiny flowers are clumped together in a raceme rather than held singly on long stems. Many family members have the ability to produce latex from a series of secretory canals. The latex can be clear, milky, orange, or in the case of bloodroot (*Sanguinaria canadensis*), blood-red. Here the sap oozes out of the cut roots just like blood from a severed finger. Some people say that 'pap' means thick milk, but others dispute that papaver may refer to the noise made when chewing the seed.

The well-known dicentra, corydalis and fumaria are also classified as Papaveraceae in *The RHS Plant Finder* although some authorities put them in a separate family: Fumariaceae. This group, unlike the other Papaveraceae, produce nectar and have watery rather than milky sap. There are many similarities, however. The complex flowers of the dicentras have four petals but they are fused in parts, especially towards the apex. The Fumariaceae also contain alkaloids but not as many as in the true Papaveraceae.

Some of the poppy family prefer moist, cool conditions whereas others relish hot, dry borders. Some gardeners go for one type, others cheat nature so they can grow them all. Whatever your preference and soil conditions, there is bound to be a member of this family to suit your border.

LEFT
Meconopsis grandis GS 600

WILD POPPIES

T HE MOST CELEBRATED of the wild poppies must be the cornfield poppy (*Papaver rhoeas*), which paints red patches on the landscape each summer. The individual flowers are short-lived and are soon followed by rounded, smooth seed capsules, but *en masse* the blooms appear to last for weeks. Although wild, the cornfield poppy generally relies on man for its survival, and is associated with cultivated land. For decades, the seeds can lie dormant in the soil waiting to be shown the sun in order to spring into life again.

The long, smooth-headed poppy (*Papaver dubium*), also has its home under the plough. It can be distinguished from the cornfield poppy by its paler red flowers and longer, smooth seed capsules. Other relations with slightly smaller flowers include the round, rough-headed poppy, (*Papaver hybridum*), with round, bristly seed capsules and the long, rough-headed poppy (*Papaver argemone*) with, as you have probably guessed, long, bristly capsules. The name *argemon* comes from the Greek for cataract, as the plant was reputed to cure cataracts of the eye. The smaller-flowered species, unlike their larger cousins, have not really made a hit in the garden, although some grow *Papaver hybridum* for its fruits, which are attractive in dried flower arrangements.

The Himalayan meconopsis are usually blue, but *Meconopsis cambrica*, the Welsh poppy, has golden yellow flowers and golden yellow sap. Meconopsis comes from the Greek *mekon*, meaning poppy, and *-opsis*, meaning likeness: 'looking like a poppy' – not very original, but true! The Welsh poppy is native to Wales,

BELOW LEFT
GREATER CELANDINE
Chelidonium majus
'Flore Pleno'

BELOW
YELLOW-HORNED POPPY
Glaucium flavum

south-west England and Ireland, occurring mainly in open woods or on rocky ground. It has been introduced elsewhere and has settled well in Scotland, having a preference for moist, damp areas. Both the native form and unusual forms, such as doubles, make good perennial garden plants for light shade. They produce flowers from spring until the first frosts and seed freely. *M. cambrica* 'Muriel Brown', a double red, is a particularly good form. It was discovered by Ray Brown of Plant World (see page 52) and was named after his mother.

Chelidonium majus, greater celandine, is a poppy too, its four-petalled, yellow flowers blooming from late spring to early autumn. Although it grows wild in Britain and northern Europe, some people believe it was introduced from southern Europe by herbalists. Its medicinal use, treating warts and gout as well as a type of tuberculosis, certainly goes back to the ancient Greek and Chinese civilizations. It is not recommended that you try these remedies as many have been disproved in recent times and others may be dangerous.

Now to the name. This is from the Greek *chelidon*, or swallow, and may be associated with the flowers which come out when the swallows arrive. The Roman naturalist Pliny suggested that it was connected with the superstition that swallows used this herb to clean the eyes of their babies. In Oxford Cathedral, a carving of *Chelidonium majus* decorates a thirteenth-century shrine to St Frideswide, benefactor of the blind and patron saint of Oxford University. However, it is not suggested for a minute that you put this plant anywhere near eyes – the sap is so toxic that it has been used to cauterize warts!

Now little used as a medicine, greater celandine has found its way into our gardens as an ornamental. Although many find it a bit weedy, it is best in wildlife areas or large woodland gardens. Many garden worthy forms are available, including *Chelidonium majus* var. *laciniatus*, with finely-divided petals and leaves, and *Chelidonium majus* 'Flore Pleno', with double flowers.

The yellow horned poppy (*Glaucium flavum*) flowers on shingle beaches from June to October. It has typical poppy-like blooms but is distinguished by its long, thin seed pods. Once again, herbals describe its use as an eye medicine, this time to remove ulcers from sheep's eyes. Glaucium and their near relations make good garden plants. Although perennial, some treat them as biennials as they need replacing every two or three years.

Corydalis and fumitory are close relations of the poppies. *Corydalis claviculata*, a climber with small creamy flowers, grows in Britain and northern Europe, but better known is common fumitory (*Fumaria officinalis*). Its old country name, God's fingers and thumbs, may relate to the delicate rose-coloured flowers which are tipped with purple. The name fumitory comes from *fumus*, smoke, and is possibly linked to the ancient exorcists who said the smoke of this plant had the power to expel evil spirits. More probable is the theory that the name stems from the smoke-like, greyish foliage which appears to curl up out of the earth.

RIGHT
COMMON POPPY
Papaver rhoeas

WILD POPPIES

GREATER CELANDINE
Chelidonium majus

CLIMBING CORYDALIS
Corydalis claviculata

COMMON FUMITORY
Fumitory officinalis

YELLOW HORNED POPPY
Glaucium flavum

WELSH POPPY
Meconopsis cambrica

LONG, ROUGH-HEADED POPPY
Papaver argemone

LONG, SMOOTH-HEADED POPPY
Papaver dubium

ROUND, ROUGH-HEADED POPPY
Papaver hybridum

ARCTIC POPPY
Papaver radicatum

CORNFIELD POPPY
Papaver rhoeas

THE FLOWERING YEAR

T HE BLOODROOT, (*Sanguinaria canadensis*), with its clusters of snow-white flowers in April and May, is one of the earliest poppies to flower. It hugs the ground and so is suited to the rock garden or front of the border. Several less well-known poppies also comes into flower at this time. *Hylomecon japonica* is a beautiful, small poppy, brightening up a woodland or shady garden with its bright-yellow flowers. In contrast comes *Dendromecon rigida*, the tree poppy. This slightly tender plant makes a large evergreen shrub, and is suited to a sheltered south wall. It has large yellow flowers which are borne sporadically between spring and autumn.

Greater celandine, *Chelidonium majus*, a rather weedy poppy, comes into bloom in May along with several near-poppy relatives: *Dicentra spectabilis*, the bleeding heart, brings soft colour to semi-shaded sites in the spring while *D. exima* brings colour to the front of the border from May to September. Corydalis also does well at the front of a shady border and comes in yellow, pink, mauve, white and blue. The blue *C. flexuosa* has become very popular and flowers from April to July, while our native *C. lutea* goes from May right through to October.

The core of the family, the bright and blowsy oriental poppies, make a real statement in May bringing huge red and pink splashes to the front and middle of the border. The revered blue meconopsis species tend to bloom at the end of the month, but there is more to this genus than meets the eye. The *Meconopsis* season actually starts in April with the rare, scarlet *M. punicea* and yellow *M. integrifolia*. When the perennial blues, including *M.* x *sheldonii*, *M. betonicifolia* and

APRIL

DESERT POPPY
Arctomecon merriamii (P)
April–May (Nevada)

TREE POPPY
Dendromecon rigida (SP)
April–September

FOREST POPPY
Hylomecon japonica (P)
April–May

BLOODROOT
Sanguinaria canadensis (P)
April–May

SARCOCAPNOS
Sarcocapnos enneaphylla (P)
April–May

WIND POPPY
Stylomecon heterophylla (A)
April–May (California)

MAY

YELLOW PYGMY POPPY
Canbya aurea (A)
May–June (Nevada)

WOODLAND POPPY
Cathcartia villosa (P)
May–June

GREATER CELANDINE
Chelidonium majus (P)
May–July

CORYDALIS
Corydalis flexuosa (P)
May–June

BLEEDING HEART
Dicentra spectabilis (P)
May–June

COMMON FUMITORY
Fumaria officinalis (A)
May–October

ORIENTAL POPPY
Papaver orientale (P)
May–June

CORNFIELD POPPY
Papaver rhoeas (A)
May–August

RUPICAPNOS
Rupicapnos africana (PA)
May–August

CELANDINE POPPY
Stylophorum diphyllum (P)
May–July

JUNE

CALIFORNIAN POPPY
Eschscholzia californica (A)
June–October

HORNED POPPY
Glaucium flavum (BP)
June–September

PLUME POPPY
Macleaya cordata (P)
June–August

HIMALAYAN BLUE POPPY
Meconopsis betonicifolia (P)
June–July

WELSH POPPY
Meconopsis cambrica (P)
June–September

OPIUM POPPY
Papaver somniferum (A)
June–August

VIOLET HORNED POPPY
Roemaria hybrida (A)
June–August

JULY

CLIMBING FUMITORY
Adlumia fungosa (B)
July–August

PRICKLY POPPY
Argemone mexicana (PA)
July–August

HIMALAYAN HORNED POPPY
Dicranostigma lactucoides (BP)
July–September (Himalayas)

SNOW POPPY
Eomecon chionanthum (P)
July–August

CALIFORNIAN TREE POPPY
Romneya x *hybrida* (P)
July–September

AUGUST

MEXICAN TULIP POPPY
Hunnemannia fumariifolia (A)
August–September

LATE MECONOPSIS
Meconopsis wallichii (HP)
August–October

M. grandis reach their peak in mid-June, they are joined by the monocarpic species: yellow *M. paniculata* and *M. napaulensis* in pink, white, yellow and scarlet. Finally in August comes *M. wallichii*, the blue or white monocarp, to fly the flag for the genus until the first frosts.

The annual poppies bring colour to all parts of the border in midsummer, blooming amongst the herbaceous plants or simply making a display of their own. The opium poppies in white, red, pink and purple give a sea of colour in the mid-border, enhanced beautifully by their pale grey-green leaves. The cornfield poppies also flower at this time, selections over the years extending the range to pinks and greys as well as the desirable scarlet. For real value for money, the prize goes to *Eschscholzia californica*, with its seemingly effortless production of masses of yellow-orange flowers from June right through to October. As with the cornfield poppies, selections have thrown up new colours: scarlet white, crimson and rose. *Glaucium flavum* brings colour to the scree or gravel garden from June to September, its blue-green foliage topped with bright yellow saucers of colour. It complements another coastal species, the summer-flowering prickly poppy, *Argemone mexicana*, also yellow but with a prickly stem. At the back of the mid- to late-summer border towers macleaya, a feathery-leaved family member with small clouds of flowers. In total contrast, the end of summer brings bold romneya, again large but with fried-egg flowers, huge and papery.

KEY
If rare in cultivation, flowering time as in native habitat.
A: annual B: biennial P: perennial S: shrub

POPPY DIRECTORY

TYPE OF PLANT	(H) HEIGHT (S) SPREAD	CONDITIONS REQUIRED (SEE KEY)	PLANT TYPE AND CULTIVATION TIP	PROPAGATION
Chelidonium majus	**H** 90 cm (3 ft) **S** 90 cm (3 ft)	◐☼◑✳✳✳	Perennial. Spreads rapidly.	Self-sown seedlings.
Corydalis flexuosa	**H** 30 cm (1 ft) **S** 30 cm (1 ft)	◐☼✳✳✳	Perennial. Likes woodland site. or peat beds.	Division when dormant.
Dicentra 'Stuart Boothman'	**H** 60 cm (2 ft) **S** 60 cm (2 ft)	◐☼◑✳✳✳	Perennial. Ground cover just about anywhere	Division in winter.
Eschscholzia californica	**H** 30 cm (1 ft) **S** 30 cm (1 ft)	◐☼✳✳✳	Annual. Sow where you want it to flower.	Seed in spring.
Glaucium flavum	**H** 30 cm (1 ft) **S** 30 cm (1 ft)	◐☼✳✳✳	Annual. Plant in gravel garden.	Sow in spring.
Macleaya cordata	**H** 1.8–2.5 m (6–8 ft) **S** 90 cm (3 ft plus)	◐☼✳✳✳	Herbaceous perennial. Requires staking.	Division or root cuttings in winter.
MECONOPSIS *Meconopsis betonicifolia*	**H** 1.2 m (4 ft) **S** 90 cm (3 ft)	◐☼✳✳✳	Herbaceous perennial Prefers woodland, peat bed.	Division in spring.
Meconopsis cambrica	**H** 30 cm (1 ft) **S** 30 cm (1 ft)	◐☼◑✳✳✳	Herbaceous perennial. Spreads rapidly.	Fresh seed sown direct.
Meconopsis grandis 'Branklyn'	**H** 1.5 m (5 ft) **S** 90 cm (3 ft)	◐☼✳✳✳	Herbaceous perennial Prefers woodland, peat bed.	Division in spring.
Meconopsis grandis GS600	**H** 1.2 m (4 ft) **S** 90 cm (3 ft)	◐☼✳✳✳	Herbaceous perennial As above.	Division in spring.
Meconopsis grandis x regia	**H** 60 cm (2 ft) **S** 60 cm (2 ft)	◐☼✳✳✳	Herbaceous perennial As above.	Division in spring.
Meconopsis napaulensis	**H** 1.8 m (6 ft) **S** 90 cm (3 ft)	◐☼✳✳✳	Monocarpic perennial. Protect rosette in winter. Peat bed.	Seed in January.
Meconopsis x sheldonii	**H** 1.2 m (4 ft) **S** 90 cm (3 ft)	◐☼✳✳✳	Herbaceous perennial Prefers woodland, peat bed.	Division in spring.

Meconopsis villosa.(syn. Cathcartia villosa)	**H** 90 cm (3 ft) **S** 90 cm (3 ft)	◐☀✹✹✹	*Herbaceous perennial. Prefers woodland, peat bed.*	*Seed or division in spring.*
PAPAVER *Papaver orientale* 'Beauty of Livermere', 'Beauty Queen'. 'Mrs Perry', 'Perry's White' 'Patty's Plum', 'Karine', 'Curlilocks'.	**H** 75-1.2 m (30 in-4 ft) **S** 60 cm (2 ft)	◌☀✹✹✹	*Deciduous herbaceous perennial. Provide twiggy supports. Cut back soon after flowering.*	*Division in spring or autumn. Cuttings of pencil-thick roots in winter.*
Papaver rhoeas 'Mother of Pearl'	**H** 90 cm (3 ft) **S** 30 cm (1 ft)	◌☀✹✹✹	*Annual. Select favourite colours to self seed.*	*Seed.*
Papaver miyabeanum	**H** 7–10 cm (3–4 in) **S** 90 cm (3 ft)	◌☀✹✹✹	*Alpine perennial. Good in scree garden.*	*Seed.*
Papaver nudicaule	**H** 30 cm (1 ft) **S** 30 cm (1 ft)	◌☀✹✹✹	*Perennial. Can treat as biennial.*	*Seed.*
Papaver rupifragum	**H** 45 cm (18 in) **S** 45 cm (18 in)	◌☀✹✹✹	*Alpine annual. Spreads rapidly in dry gardens.*	*Seed usually self sown.*
Papaver somniferum	**H** 1.5 m (5 ft) **S** 30 cm (1 ft)	◌☀✹✹✹	*Annual. Can become a weed.*	*Seed.*
Romneya x *hybrida*	**H** 1.8 m (6 ft) plus **S** 1.8 m (6 ft) plus	◌☀✹✹	*Herbaceous perennial. Resents root disturbance.*	*Seed or root cuttings.*
Sanguinaria canadensis 'Flore Plena'	**H** 30 cm (1 ft) **S** 60 cm (2 ft)	◐☀✹✹✹	*Herbaceous perennial . Likes peat bed or moist rockery.*	*Division in spring.*

KEY
◌ Well drained soil ◐ Moist soil ● Wet soil ☀ Sun ☀ Partial shade ✹ Tolerates full shade
✹ Half-hardy to 0°C (32°F) ✹✹ Frost-hardy to -5°C (23°F) ✹✹✹ Fully hardy to -15°C (5°F)

THE GARDENS
CRAIGIEBURN POPPIES

Revered by most gardeners, Himalayan blue poppies have a teasing reputation for fussiness. To succeed with meconopsis, an understanding of their natural habitat is essential. Short of visiting the Himalayas, the best option is an early summer trip to Craigieburn, Bill Chudziak's garden near Moffat in Scotland.

THE AIR AT CRAIGIEBURN is so fresh that a southerner like me could get high on it. The Craigieburn itself runs just above the 3.2 hectare (8 acre) garden, crashing over boulders and energizing the air. Imagine a gentle hillside with the garden nestled into the slope, so frosts float over the trees without lingering. This shelter, and a slight warming effect from the Gulf Stream, creates almost ideal growing conditions for the National Collection of meconopsis.

Most gardeners start by wanting to grow the perennial blue-flowered species like *M. grandis*. Standing by an impressive clump, Bill explained why they flourish in his garden. 'Most of the meconopsis spend their lives in the clouds. Here at Craigieburn, the climate approximates to that of the cool moisture-laden Himalayan valleys, say, at about 4,000 m (13,000 ft). Our rainfall is 1.9 m (75 in) a year, and any garden with less must compensate in some way.'

Choose the coolest place in your garden, and prepare the soil well. Bill explained their greed for organic matter. 'George Sheriff, the great Himalayan

LEFT
*Meconopsis villosa
(syn. Cathcartia
villosa)*

RIGHT
BLUE POPPY
*Meconopsis grandis
GS 600*

plant hunter, recommended planting meconopsis on top of a dead sheep'. More practical alternatives are vast quantities of well-rotted manure, garden compost or leaf mould. 'The best time to plant is early spring,' said Bill. 'Put them about 60 cm (2 ft) apart, and plant as many as you can get hold of. They create their own microclimate and flower better in company. Don't mollycoddle them or give them any protection. Remember, they are the children of the hills.'

Although there are glades of meconopsis in the garden, the 150 varieties which comprise the National Collection are grown in nursery beds. 'It is largely a scientific collection, aimed at conservation and comparison,' said Bill. 'Many meconopsis hover on the fringes of cultivation, and this ensures their survival.'

Craigieburn is a brand new garden, created on an old site. 'We began in late 1989 with a chainsaw and a machete, cutting out decades of self-sown brambles and rhododendrons,' said Bill. 'Only mature trees were left, but we have since added over 5,000 varieties of plants. Meconopsis are just a fraction of the picture.'

Of the many wonderful poppies in the garden, Bill singled out *M. villosa* (syn. *Cathcartica villosa*), a perennial yellow which frequently flowers twice and sets copious seed – a good plant. A current excitement is a stunning violet *M. betonicifolia* 'Hensoll Violet', newly acquired from a garden in Galloway. 'We hybridize experimentally ourselves, but also look out for new forms, either from the wild or from other gardens. We are usually able to sort out muddles over nomenclature, and liaise closely with the RHS. '

But Bill's greatest love is the monocarpic species. In their first few years they make giant rosettes of hairy leaves, until a final burst of energy pushes up a candelabra-like flower spike, after which they seed and die. Bill reckons them to be the test of the true meconopsis fanatic and for him, the pinnacle of the genus is *M. superba*. Huge, felted silver rosettes culminate in spikes of delicate white flowers, centred with a prominent black stigma. They are desirable and difficult, needing protection from winter wet. Easier are the forms of *M. napaulensis*, with flowers of white, yellow, pink, or even a glossy claret. One oddity is a cross between *M. betonicifolia* and *M. x napaulensis* called *Meconopsis* 'James Cobb'. It looks like a monocarpic meconopsis, but is fully perennial.

Bill loves all poppies, but has had to compensate to grow the 'hot poppies'. Orange *Papaver rupifragum* seeds itself around a well-drained raised bed, and the annual horned poppy *Glaucium corniculatum* enjoys the south-facing slope of the autumn garden. Prickly American argemones and eschscholzias are sown directly into gravel paths where they flourish among osteospermums and rock roses.

There is an excitement in the air here, partly explained by the shimmering blue of the poppies and the energy created by rejuvenation. Bill makes no secret of the hold it has on him. 'Although I am head gardener at Craigieburn, it is also my home. It is, quite simply, the best place in the world.'

ORIENTAL POPPIES

On the day Anne Swithinbank visited Jane Lipington's allotment on the outskirts of Bath, the weather was bleak and rainy. Clouds swirled over nearby Solsbury Hill, but they failed to douse the bright colours of her oriental poppies. Their amazing blooms, blousy yet fragile, bring a touch of glamour to early summer.

ALTHOUGH SOME OTHER allotment holders in the area were growing a few flowers on their plots, mainly for cutting or to attract beneficial insects, Jane's stood out like a beacon. 'I haven't got room for them in my tiny garden,' she explained, 'but I have built up this collection and plan to start a nursery. I really think these poppies are due for a revival and deserve to be more popular.' She may be right: a peek into the plant crèches at flower shows is always revealing, and last year I could see quite a few orientals waving like huge silky flags from visitor's shopping bags.

There are only about 60 different cultivars of oriental poppies available and Jane, a horticulturist who specializes in the provision of training for women gardeners, has 35 of them. All are striking, but I picked out apricot 'Karine' as a favourite, although Jane's is fringe-petalled 'Curlilocks'. It is immensely showy, with shiny red laciniated petals marked with black blotches at the centre.

Oriental poppies are a mixture of two distinct but closely allied species,

LEFT
Papaver orientale

RIGHT
Papaver orientale
'Curlilocks'

LEFT
Papaver orientale
'Perry's White'

RIGHT
Papaver orientale
'Beauty Queen'

P. bracteatum and *P. orientale*, with a shared origin in Turkey and other nearby countries. These wild poppies bear red flowers and flourish in the stony soil of mountainside meadows. Jane showed me how to tell which parent was most dominant in some of the varieties she grows. Dark red 'Beauty of Livermere' has a lot of *P. bracteatum* in its parentage. 'To begin with, it has bracts,' said Jane, pointing out the small green structures beneath the petals. 'There are oblong marks inside the flower and the plant is tall, at around 1.2 m (4 ft), with a stiff, upright habit, which also means its stems are good for cutting.'

A nearby orange-flowered cultivar was closer to *P. orientale*. 'There are no bracts, the blotch in the middle of each petal is square or rounded and it has a more lax habit,' Jane pointed out. Oriental poppies need careful siting in gardens. 'If you're not careful, they tend to flop all over other plants, although it is possible to support them. Fortunately, the foliage dies off soon after flowering, so it can be cut back. The trick is to grow them alongside later-flowering herbaceous perennials that can take over to fill the gaps.'

The colour range of pinks, oranges, white and reds in oriental poppies has only been available from 1906, when nurseryman Amos Perry found a colour break among his red-flowered seedlings. He named this pink-flowered poppy after his wife, and 'Mrs Perry' is still available today. Excited by this break, Amos tried to encourage even paler colours by hand-pollinating the flowers and carefully sowing the seed, but the results were all red-flowered plants. The story of how 'Perry's White' finally came about is told by his daughter-in-law Frances Perry in her book, *The World of Flowers*. In 1912, Amos sold some supposedly scarlet poppies to a client for a special colour-themed border. A year later the client was up in arms because his scheme had been ruined by a white-flowered poppy. Amos went to the garden, exchanged the poppy for other plants and then took away what became 'Perry's White'. Since then, other cultivars have arisen from seedlings almost by accident.

When Jane does start a nursery, she will find it easy to increase her stock, as oriental poppies are easy to propagate. 'The simplest method is by division,' she said. 'Plants can be lifted in autumn or spring, their roots divided and the portions replanted.' If many plants are needed, root cuttings are the answer. 'Lift a plant in late summer and find lengths of roots the thickness of a pencil. Cut them into sections 4-5 cm (just under 2 in) long, keeping them the correct way up. Prepare a 10-12 cm (4-5 in) pot of cuttings compost (50:50 sharp sand and loam) and insert four or five upright cuttings, so that they are just covered. Put them in a coldframe with a little bottom heat if possible, and they will root in three to four weeks. Leave them for a few months, then pot singly in late spring. They can be planted out the following autumn and should flower the next year.'

I already grow a couple of different oriental poppies in my borders at home, but came away wanting more. They bear the most magnificent flowers and their seed capsules are attractive, too, the petals falling to leave a rounded pod crowned with a velvety top. Seed pods can be dried and kept, or just removed. If left on, the seeds eventually shake out and will germinate in their thousands. 'Fortunately, they are easy to hoe off,' said Jane. 'Plants can be grown from seed, but of course the results will be variable.'

PLANTSMAN'S CHOICE

BILL CHUDZIAK

PAPAVER RHOEAS

When man first cultivated the land and planted cereals, the scarlet field poppy settled down alongside. *Papaver rhoeas* is a weed of cultivated ground, lighting up arable land from western Asia to western Europe with galaxies of shimmering scarlet flowers, a constant element in man's annual struggle to grow his daily bread. Modern herbicides may have given the farmer the upper hand of late, but although poppies might appear to retreat, they never disappear completely.

So why is this cornfield weed so persistently successful? Firstly, it is exceptionally prolific; one plant alone can produce 17,000 seeds of long viability. If necessary they can sit for decades below the ground, but as soon as the soil is turned over, exposure to light triggers germination. The annual corn-growing routine dovetails perfectly with their lifecycle, and they have moved with farmers to colonize the wheatfields of Canada and Australia.

Where the fertile plains of northern France and Belgium were ravaged by the terrible battles of the First World War, they sprang out of the bruised earth in their millions, and their scarlet petals have come to stand for the blood of all those killed in two world wars. Three thousand years ago, Homer likened the drooping head of a dying warrior to a poppy flower bowed down by rain, so the battlefield connection is an ancient one.

The great art critic John Ruskin loved poppies and described them brilliantly: 'It is an intensely simple, intensely floral flower. All silk and flame ... you cannot have a more complete, a more stainless type of flower absolute; inside and out, all flower. No sparing of colour anywhere – no outside coarseness – no interior secrecies; open as the sunshine that creates it.'

There are some desirable seed strains and selections. 'Ladybird', scarlet with black blotches, is scintillating. 'Mother-of-Pearl' strain, ruthlessly selected by the great artist-plantsman Sir Cedric Morris, is a shimmering mixture of subtle pastels, including an opalescent lavender-grey of great beauty. Nothing, however, surpasses the high summer glory of a wheatfield ablaze with scarlet poppies.

LEFT
CORNFIELD POPPY *Papaver rhoeas*

RIGHT
Papaver rhoeas 'Mother of Pearl'

SANGUINARIA CANADENSIS 'PLENA'

One of my spring rituals is to make a daily inspection of a patch of peaty soil shaded by a birch tree. Here grows a colony of one of my favourite members of my favourite plant family, the double form of the Canadian bloodroot, *Sanguinaria canadensis* 'Plena'. Its first appearance is one of the red-letter days of spring. Putty-coloured shoots like little mushrooms push purposefully through the loose soil, and within days each of these blunt nubs unfurls to reveal a leaf neatly enfolding a flower bud. Each leaf is generously scalloped around the margin, and each undulation is itself daintily scalloped, a most unusual and elegant shape. The colour is green overlaid with pewter, and the reverse of the leaf is frosted with white down. They are, for me, among the most beautiful in the garden.

The flowers, too, are glorious, double, but not overly so. Although the petals are plentiful, the flower shape is both defined and refined, never descending into overblown muddle. The colour is pure

BLOODROOT
Sanguinaria canadensis 'Plena'

JAPANESE POPPY
Papaver miyabeanum

OPIUM POPPY
Papaver somniferum (seed heads)

unsullied white, and the effect is of small double waterlilies floating serenely over pools of grey-green foliage. The flowers are borne in succession, and although its season is short, it is one of the brightest performers of the spring garden, a veritable star among stars.

It grows from slowly creeping rhizomes, and these ooze blood-red sap if damaged or cut, which is, of course, where the common name comes from. In America it is also called the red puckoon, a name which has me stumped.

Give it a close approximation of its native conditions, with cool humus-rich soil in semi-shade, and cultivate the personal virtue of patience, as clumps are slow to build. The reward is one of the most sublime little plants we can grow in our gardens.

PAPAVER MIYABEANUM

This appealing little poppy is a welcome newcomer in our gardens, but is already widely available either in plant or seed form. It produces a miniature mound of tufted grey foliage, intricately divided and lobed. The flower stems are seldom more than 7-10 cm (3-4 in) high, and are topped by pale sulphur-yellow flowers with matching stamens. They are perfectly in scale with the tiny plant, classic poppy flower writ small. There is a white form which is almost as delightful. I particularly like flowers of that pale moonlight yellow which is in such perfect harmony with the glaucous leaves, and so the type plant is my favourite. But I grow both forms with great pleasure. The seed capsules are plump with a prominent flat stigmatic disc; they resemble tiny green toffee-apples, and greatly add to the decorative value of the entire plant.

Papaver miyabeanum comes from the Kurile islands north of Japan. Its diminutive size places it firmly among the treasures of the rock garden where sharp drainage and a dry crown are important if it is to flourish. Failing an open rock garden situation, or better still, a scree bed, give it a privileged position on a trough. Add extra grit to the soil, and place it in an open sunny spot. It tends to be short-lived, and our mild wet winters often finish it off, but be vigilant when you tidy up around the remains the following spring. There are always a few seedlings to perpetuate the succession. It germinates readily, but the seedlings are horribly apt to damp off. The answer is to avoid mollycoddling. Cover the seedpans with grit and sow the seed thinly onto this. Stand them outside, and do not fuss over the seedlings. Enjoy a colony of this exquisite and luminous little Japanese poppy.

PAPAVER SOMNIFERUM

Opium poppies, *Papaver somniferum*, are the very essence of the romantic summer garden, elbowing their way up through the roses, or self-sowing happily through the borders. Beautiful in themselves, they also impart great atmosphere into the garden, a sort of brimming romantic abundance, and, being annuals they also have that fragile ephemeral quality which makes us value them all the more. Dutch flower painters loved them and used them as an element in those great floral extravaganzas which were all the rage during the seventeenth century. They took care to capture the moment of petal-fall, reminding us of our own mortality. Thus the fleeting beauty of the opium poppy was taken to represent the brevity of human life.

The large undulating leaves are cool and hairless, blue-green with a smooth bloom. A well-grown plant can reach 1.5 m (5 ft), but is very narrow so fits neatly in gaps between neighbours. One characteristic it shares with most poppies is the surprising bud-to-petal ratio. When the great billows and flounces of petal are released, it seems utterly impossible that they should ever have fitted into the encasing bud. In fact the flower must be packed away just like a parachute, all folded and concertinaed, and it bears the creases of its confinement until ironed out by the sun. The petals are like silk or chiffon, and come in a huge range of colours, from white and yellow through to black; only blue is missing. Many of the singles have dark blotches at the base of the petals and are very beautiful, but the real glories are the doubles, often called peony-flowered poppies. Here at Craigieburn in mid-July we have several types in flower – a double pink with fringed and fimbriated petals, a drift of double whites ('Swansdown') which are presently floating around our autumn garden, recreating the last act of *Giselle,* and a mean lipstick-red with a black basal blotch. Best of all, though, are the astounding double blacks in our rose garden. These are quite wicked, with frilled double flowers of darkest aubergine. The petals are shiny – not a superficial slick shine, but a deep and subtle sheen, like Chinese lacquer. Sensational.

Opium poppies have been cultivated by man since Neolithic times, and were known as a sedative by the ancient Greeks. Arab pharmacists called the plant '*abu el noum*', the father of sleep, and it was grown throughout the Arab empire as a narcotic and medicinal herb. In Shakespeare, 'poppy' is a synonym for sedative. It was at the heart of the Opium Wars of the nineteenth century in which Britain forced China to continue, against the will of its government, to buy opium produced in British India. The plant contains powerful alkaloids which are the basis not only of opium and heroin, but of many modern hospital drugs, which are analgesic, sedative or anti-spasmodic. These are derived not from the seeds but from the latex. The golden triangle of northern Burma, Thailand and south-west China is the heart of the international illegal drugs trade; in Tasmania, opium poppies are farmed legally.

RIGHT

OPIUM POPPY *Papaver somniferum*

It is perfectly legal to grow them in gardens, and our climate, in any case, is not hot enough to produce the necessary opiates in the resin. Their cultivation is simplicity itself. Just scatter the seed where you want the plants, and it will germinate. It will also perpetuate by self-sowing. Any good seed catalogue will offer several mouth-watering varieties. Every garden, from the grandest to the tiniest plot, should grow this wonderful plant.

ESCHSCHOLZIA CALIFORNICUM

The garden writer Graham Rice calls this an 'unspellable little annual', and I wonder how many gardeners omit it from the seed order because the prospect of spelling it causes brain shutdown. Others turn their noses up at what they regard as an unsophisticated sort of plant: a garish seed packet that comes taped onto a magazine cover, or sits with the other cheap and cheerful subjects in the local supermarket. But, please, take the trouble to grow it. Look at it with fresh eyes, and I am sure that you will find it as endearing as I do.

The wild plant colonizes dry and stony places in the hills of California and southern Oregon – its more manageable name is 'Californian poppy'. It first produces a mound of finely dissected foliage of a refined and beautiful sea-green. Next, strange little conical buds appear. Then emerge the wide funnel-shaped flowers, and refinement is thrown to the winds. They are satin-textured, and flauntingly intense in colour, being predominately vibrant orange or pure primary yellow. A minority are cream, and these have been used to dilute the stronger colours resulting in a range of apricots, salmons, and pinks. Reds and bronzes have resulted from selections. Other innovations have frilled petals, or are semi-double, or bicolors, but I prefer the bright simple elegance of the wild type. Elongated seed pods add a final decorative element.

Growing it is easy. Just scatter the seed where you want it to grow, and wait. Never be tempted to pamper it by giving it bedding-plant treatment; transplanting is usually terminal. In our cool damp climate we try to replicate life on the sierra by sowing direct into the gravel drive. And if you feel yourself too grand to grow it, remember that Vita Sackville-West, doyenne of horticultural good taste, cherished this dazzling little plant.

MACLEAYA CORDATA

This stately giant from China or Japan is a most unpoppy-like poppy. But by some curious twist – and this is what makes classification by family so intriguing – it bears a marked resemblance to the Canadian bloodroot, *Sanguinaria canadensis*. On paper, this seems unlikely. Macleaya reaches 1.8-2.5 m (6-8 ft) in height, originates from the Far East, and carries great feathery panicles of tiny flowers. Its common name, indeed, is plume poppy. Sanguinaria, on the other hand, is barely 30 cm (1 ft) tall, hails from the New

World, and has relatively large cup-shaped flowers. Two things, however, immediately indicate close kinship. Both share an exceptionally beautiful leaf, grey-green above, white below, and prominently veined with white. Although those of macleaya are heart-shaped, and those of sanguinaria kidney-shaped, each has the delicate scalloped leaf-edge, and bears a striking resemblance to the other. Each, moreover, bleeds bright orange-red sap when wounded. Did they evolve separately, or do they share a common ancestor? We can only speculate.

Macleaya cordata is so beautiful of leaf that, despite its towering stature, it should be placed where it can be seen in its entirety, in large architectural clumps fringing a lawn, for instance. If you want it in your borders, be sure to avoid the similar *Macleaya microcarpa*, with its rampantly invasive rootstock, in favour of the much better-mannered *Macleaya cordata*. The foamy flower panicles are creamy buff, lovely against a dark background, but there are also named cultivars, such as 'Flamingo', a soft buff-pink. A reasonably fertile soil in full sun suits it best, and a mulch of organic matter in autumn doubles both as nutrition, and protection. I love big bold plants, and this is one of the best, a joy from its first appearance in spring to its final collapse with the onset of frost.

ROMNEYA COULTERI

These giant Californian tree poppies are unrivalled in the garden for high-impact pizzazz. Great sea-green woody stems rocket up to 2.5 m (8 ft) in a single season, crowned by enormous white flowers, fully 12 cm (5 in) across. These magnificent flowers open almost flat, but their crimped and pleated petals and frilled edges give them an air of delicacy, despite their blatant size. Like many poppies, the number of petals is by no means constant; some flowers have five or six, some only four, but each is centred by a dense boss of showy golden stamens surrounding a prominent stigma. The flowers, usually singly-borne, are succeeded by bristly golden ovoid seed capsules. The foliage, too, is decorative, being airily divided and coolly glaucous, a perfect foil for the pale luminous flowers.

Technically the plant is a sub-shrub from the sun-baked hillsides of California, but in our cooler climate it frequently behaves as a herbaceous perennial. Many gardeners feel it must be unsuited to the rigours of the British climate, but, given good drainage, it seems unaffected by low temperatures and drizzle. Indeed one of the best colonies I know is in less-than-sun-drenched Perthshire.

It is, however, a beast of a plant to get established. Many gardeners have resorted to ordering plants wholesale, and siting them in both likely and unlikely positions. It might languish for years before dying

RIGHT

CALIFORNIAN POPPY *Eschscholzia* 'Special Mix'

out, but if it does decide to flourish, then beware! It has spectacularly loutish tendencies, ramping through your borders, pushing up your tarmac drive, and even sending triffid-like suckers up through your kitchen lino. E.A. Bowles condemned it as 'stingy old curmudgeon in its views about providing flowers', but one of the happier results of recent long hot summers has been our ability to flower these glorious sun-lovers in our gardens.

DICENTRA

Two hundred ago, *Dicentra formosa* was introduced from North America, where it grows in the great Redwood and Sequoia-dendron forests of the west coast ranges. It quickly settled down in our climate, and has even naturalized in many areas. It is a gentle colonizer, marching ever outwards from a fleshy creeping rootstock to form a feathery carpet in the loose woodland soil which is its preferred medium. The foliage is beautiful, deeply divided and fern-like, and in some cultivars – like 'Stuart Boothman' – the leaves are pale pewter-green. Its first random flowers are out with the hellebores, but it really gets underway in April, and from then on

flowers lavishly until midsummer. The flower stems are hairless and translucent, often suffused with chestnut-brown. Clusters of narrow flowers dangle from the down-turned tips of the stems. They are typically mauvy-pink, paler in 'Stuart Boothman', but ranging through to claret in the recent and desirable 'Bacchanal'. There are also white forms, of which the best is 'Langtrees', also known as 'Pearl Drops'. Each small flower is roughly heart-shaped, but being clearly bifurcated, or forked, it always reminds me of an extravagantly baggy pair of tiny jodhpurs.

Dicentra formosa and its cultivars are easily grown in cool dampish conditions. In warmer climates they are best sited in shade, and might suffer a touch of mildew in prolonged dry weather. They are wonderful colonizing light woodland, and combine particularly well with the dark crimson leaves of *Euphorbia amygdaloides*, and also the glaucous leaves and apple-green flowers of *Helleborus corsicus*. They seem to thrive with *Symphytum* species (comfrey), even in dry shade under trees.

Since their introduction into cultivation, dicentras have sheltered under the umbrella of the poppy family. Recently, however, taxonomists have been guided by common sense, and the genus has now joins corydalis and fumitories in the Fumariaceae.

BELOW

PLUME POPPY *Macleaya cordata*

CORYDALIS FLEXUOSA

This plant is relatively new in cultivation, having been introduced from western China in 1989. In less than ten years it has swept out through garden centres, and there can scarcely be a keen gardener in the land who does not grow it. It is a pretty and dainty plant with filmy fern-like foliage, lightly tinged with bronze. The flowers, carried in delicate sprays, are tubular with an upswept spur, and they weave around like shoals of small blue fish. Like the dicentras, it is in the Fumariaceae family, whose kinship with the poppies is so close that taxonomists divided the two genera only fairly recently.

In its native Sichuan it grows in the moist leaf litter of the shady forest floor, so these are the conditions to replicate in the garden. In the cool damp areas of north and west Britain, corydalis grow virtually anywhere, self-seeding abundantly, but in drier hotter gardens they need to be placed in a moist corner, beside a shady drain, or in a north border, if they are to flourish. Summer heat induces dormancy, although in a damp autumn a second crop of leaves and flowers often appear.

There are several strains, each with a different clonal name. 'China Blue' had good true-blue flowers, though all flower colour is more intense and longer lasting in cool conditions. 'Purple Leaf' has a glaucous leaf when young, and is the smallest clone. 'Pere David' is also bronze-leaved, and has the largest flowers, while 'Blue Panda' is supposed to be the best all-round form. *Corydalis flexuosa* is prolific and easy to propagate, the rhizomes breaking up into scores of tiny rice-like nubs, each of which develops into a new plant. I value it, and feel it to be the harbinger of many wonderful corydalis yet to be introduced from China.

Even more desirable is the lovely *Corydalis cashmeriana* from the Himalayas. Close racemes of lapis-lazuli blue flowers hover over delicate and finely-dissected foliage. The general effect is exquisite and jewel-like. I have seen this plant growing wild at 4500 m (15,000 ft), where it wandered through the Himalayan fern *Dryopteris wallichiana*, gentians, and *Bergenia purpurescens*. Here, it could not tolerate such rough company, but would need the coolness and shelter of a shady peat-bed.

If *Corydalis ochroleuca* came from the Himalayas and was quite difficult to grow, then everybody would be clamouring to get hold of it. It has the same maidenhair fern foliage as the asiatic species, and racemes of creamy flowers delicately tipped with lemon. Distinctive and appealing, it is also obliging, seeding happily around to colonize any bare areas among other plants in the garden. It will even appear between the cracks in old walls but, although prolific, this plant is never unwelcome or invasive. Unwanted seedlings can be removed easily, but because I rate it so highly, I tend to leave them all.

TREE POPPY
Romneya coulteri

Dicentra 'Stuart Boothman'

Corydalis flexuosa

FLORISTRY

LYNDSAY HART

HELICHRYSUM

Dried flower arrangements can include a surprising range of flowers that may be easily dried at home, from the seed heads of the humble kitchen chive to the stately spires of the delphinium. Among the daisy family, artichokes and sunflowers make spectacular dried statements, but in a family full of classic everlasting flowers, the most famous are the helichrysums. Familiarity may have bred a certain contempt for these old favourites, yet with careful use their inclusion in a dried arrangement can add a special form and depth of colour. In late summer, fresh helichrysums can be purchased very cheaply from many flower shops. Buy while still in bud, wire heads and stems then hang bunches upside down in a warm dark place, ready to use a few weeks later. Completed dried arrangements should be placed away from direct sunlight, which will fade colours

LEFT *Helichrysum*
BELOW **SWEET PEA** *Lathyrus odoratus*

quickly. Although helichrysums are indeed everlasting, it is best to think of them, like all dried flowers, as having their own season. Warm, subtle tints in winter can look stale in summer – better to start each autumn with new and exciting displays for a fresh season.

SWEET PEAS

Cut flowers are now imported from around the world, and we have become used to buying many summer flowers, even in the depths of winter – but not the delicate sweet pea (*Lathyrus odoratus*). These beautiful, fragile blooms do not travel well, making it almost impossible for other countries to compete with domestic growers. Nearly all our sweet peas are grown in England and their season is relatively short, from May to perhaps the end of July.

Most sweet peas sold in florist shops have been treated with a solution that inhibits the production of ethylene, a natural gas found in fruit and flowers which causes them to mature and decay. This means that florists' varieties should last much longer than those

picked from the garden. Shop-bought flowers should have their stems re-cut and placed in deep water for a while. Cut from the garden, they should last at least four or five days in water. Pick in the cool of the morning or evening, selecting flowers where the top bud is just showing colour.

Sweet peas can be arranged with other flowers, but look lovely in a vase on their own. Avoid putting too many in one container as this makes them die more rapidly and, although they will not last as long as carnations or chrysanthemums, a few days' vase life is a small sacrifice for such a heavenly sight and scent.

PERSIAN BUTTERCUPS

There is something magical about Persian buttercups *(Ranunculus asiaticus)*. From deepest crimson, scarlet, tawny orange and pink to glistening yellow and white, it is hard to think of another flower that could provide such a dazzling range of colours.

Although undervalued as a cut flower, perhaps because of their delicate appearance, in water they will usually last more than a week. They even manage to die beautifully, the petals becoming crispy and translucent, turning their colours to softer, muted shades. Spring is the season for home-grown varieties, and the season is

extended from late October to May by Dutch growers and the Italian growers of San Remo and Naples, who produce single-coloured and double varieties. Some of the foreign-grown flowers, bred by the Japanese, have flowerheads so densely packed with petals that they resemble old-fashioned cabbage roses.

When buying, check that the leaves are not yellowing, re-cut stems and strip away the bottom leaves before placing in water. For flowers with very heavy heads and hollow stems, insert a florist's wire up through the stem to hold the head in position. Like most members of the Ranunculaceae family, they are great drinkers, so water levels should be maintained.

MINT TUSSIE-MUSSIES

Ideal ingredients for an old-fashioned tussie-mussie are the uniquely aromatic plants of the mint family, many of which dry extremely well while retaining their scent. The origins of the word are obscure but historically these aromatic posies, made from medicinal plants, had a very practical purpose – to disguise odours and help protect their owners from plague and disease.

Materials can include many herbs found in the garden: sage, lavender, rosemary, mint and ballota. Of course, plants outside the mint family can be included – perhaps a rose for colour and perfume, or indeed any flower that dries well.

BELOW **ICELAND POPPY** *Papaver nudicaule*

To make a tussie-mussie, cut all the stems to uniform length and strip the bottom leaves from the stalks. Select an eye-catching bloom for the central focal point, then around it arrange a circlet of different material, perhaps purple sage or lavender, ensuring the tops of the leaves are level with the central bloom. Continue building up with rows of contrasting foliage and flowers until complete, then tie off with raffia or perhaps some velvet ribbon. Use fresh or, better still, hang up to dry, for the tussie-mussie will retain its perfume for many months.

LILIES

Most of the lilies we buy as cut flowers come from Holland, where growers have introduced an almost bewildering number of new hybrids. Among the larger pink hybrids are the lovely 'Le Reve', and the most beautiful oriental hybrids like 'Pissaro' and 'Berlin'. Classic white lilies include the heavily scented 'Casa Blanca' and the elegant Easter lily *(L. longiflorum)*.

When buying, check that leaves are green and not yellowing, and the flowers are still in bud, with a little colour showing. Strip away leaves that will be below water level, re-cut stems and plunge into deep water. Removing stamens as the flowers open prevents pollen staining clothes and furniture, and helps the blooms last longer.

Containers overflowing with tulips or anemones can look wonderful, but an over-filled vase of lilies may appear tousled. With such strong, bold lines it is more effective for each flower to define its own space; one stem may have greater impact then ten. Even in season lilies are not cheap, but their elegant blooms last longer than almost any other flower.

ICELAND POPPIES

Native to the lands of ice, the tundra regions of northern Norway, Russia and Canada, Icelandic poppies are a hardy race from which many lovely hybrids have been created. Their appearance does not reflect their origins: shimmering tissue-paper petals held on slim naked stems look as though they will collapse in the slightest breeze. However, while most varieties of garden poppies will last only a day or two in water, the Iceland will keep for well over a week after picking, and make a wonderful cut flower.

Cut the stems in the evening before the flower opens, when the stem has straightened but the flower bud is still shut, with no colour showing. Dip the ends of the stems in boiling water to release the air-lock within, keeping in water only as long as bubbles emerge from the stem and holding the flower and rest of the stem away from the steam. Plunge the stems into cold water, then for best effect arrange simply in a container on their own.

RIGHT **PERSIAN BUTTERCUP** *Ranunculus asiaticus*

PLANT NAMES AND CLASSIFICATION

In all, there are about 250,000 species of flowering plants, each with their own unique design to attain the same goal. Back in the early eighteenth century, as more and more of these species were discovered, the system of naming plants fell into chaos. Classification was quite arbitrary, based on facts such as where the plants grew and if they were edible or poisonous. Often they were given different names by different botanists, some of them 20 or 30 words long! Fortunately a Swedish physician, Carl Linnaeus, made a breakthrough and devised a concise system of classifying plants. A great cataloguer, he not only gave each plant a long descriptive name, but also an abbreviated two-word name, a binomial, and published his work in his *Species Plantarum* (1753). He also placed plants into larger family groups based on the number and position of the sexual parts of their flowers.

Linnaeus's work was attacked by many of his contemporaries, but eventually they adopted the binominal system as it worked. The larger groupings caused more problems. However, Linnaeus battled on with plant and animal classifications for as long as he could, and eventually died in 1778.

Today we still use the basis of Linnaeus's binomial naming system, but his larger 'sexual system' has been superseded. Taxonomy is now based on all the plant parts, even at a chemical and genetic level. However, for the layperson, the general flower structure is still a valuable way to tell which family a plant belongs to.

Plant families are further subdivided into genera and species, so each plant has its own name, which can be recognized anywhere in the world.

The genus name is a little like a surname, and the species name is akin to a forename. Plant names are taken a step further; where one or more of the species is just that little bit different from the others, it is sometimes given varietal status. If man has intervened it is given cultivar (cultivated variety) status.

For example, in the case of our common garden daisy:
Family: Compositae.
Genus: *Bellis*.
Species: *perennis*.
Cultivars: 'Alba Plena', 'Alice', 'Annie', 'Dawn Raider', and so on.
Common name: daisy.

As with all families, flowers have their fair share of black sheep. The paeony, for example, was once classed as a member of the buttercup family but was thrown out and placed in a family of its own, the Paeoniaceae. As W J Bean so eloquently puts it in the preface to *Trees and Shrubs Hardy in the British Isles* (1st edition), 'The question of nomenclature is always a vexed one. The only thing certain is, that it is impossible to please everyone.'

Plant names continue to be changed as our knowledge grows, but for simplicity and clarity a single reference work has been selected for this book. As it is for gardeners, and gardeners are always after new plants, the classification found in *The RHS Plant Finder* (1996/1997) edition is used, complying with the RHS Advisory panel on Nomenclature and Taxonomy.

CONTACTS

Alpine Garden Society
AGS Centre, Avon Bank
Pershore, Worcester WR10 3JP

Avon Bulbs
Burnt House Farm
Mid Lambrook
South Petherton
Somerset TA13 5HE

British Clematis Society
The Tropical Bird Gardens
Rode, Avon BA3 6QW

Cairngrow Lilies
Woodburn, Kinnaird Road
Westown, Carde of Gowrie
Perthshire PH2 7SU

Cambridge Botanical Gardens
Cory Lodge, Bateman St.
Cambridge CB2 1JF

Chelsea Physic Garden
66 Royal Hospital Road
London SW3 4HS

M. Oviatt-Ham Clematis
15 Green Street, Willingham
Cambridgeshire CB4 5JA

The Cottage Garden Society
5 Nixon Close, Thornhill
Dewsbury
West Yorkshire WF12 0JA

Craigieburn Classic Plants
Craigieburn House, Moffat
Dumfrieshire DG10 9LF

The Delphinium Society
Takakkaw, Ice House Wood
Oxted, Surrey RH8 9DW

English Nature
Northminster House
Peterborough PE1 1UA

Folley Farm Nursery
Bourton on Water
GL54 3BY

Glebe Cottage Plants
Pixie Lane, Warkleigh
Umberleigh
Devon EX37 9DH

Hardy's Cottage Garden Plants
The Walled Garden
Laverstock Park, Whitchurch
Hants RG28 7NT

Hiley's Nursery
25 Little Woodcote Estate
Telegraph Track
Wallington, Surrey SN5 4AU

Home Meadows Nursery Ltd
Top Street, Martlesham
Woodbridge
Suffolk IP12 4RD

Jekka's Herb Farm
Rose Cottage, Shellards Lane
Alveston
Bristol BS12 2SY

Lathyrus Information Exchange
Weaver's Cottage
35 Streetly End
West Wickham
Cambridge CB1 6RP

Lizzie's Flower Shop
78 High Street
Beckenham
Kent BR3 1ED

National Chrysanthemum Society
8 Amber Business Village
Amber Close, Tamworth
Staffordshire B77 4RD

National Gardens Scheme
Hatchlands Park
East Clandon, Guildford
Surrey GU4 7RT

NCCPG
The Pines c/o Wisley Gardens
Woking, Surrey GU23 6QB

Norwood Hall
Ealing Tertiary College
Norwood Green
Southall, Middx. UB2 4LA

Parham Park
Parham House
Pulborough RH20 4HS

Plant World
St. Marychurch Road
Newton Abbot
Devon TQ12 4SE

RHS Lily Group
c/o Rosemary Cottage
Lobands, Redmarley
Gloucestershire GL19 3NG

RHS Rosemoor Gardens
Greater Torrington
Devon EX38 8PH

RHS Wisley Gardens
Woking
Surrey GU23 6QB

Rougham Hall Nurseries
Ipswich Road, Rougham
Bury St. Edmunds
Suffolk IP30 9LE

Rowden Gardens Nursery
Brentnor, Tavistock
Devon DL19 0NG

Royal Botanic Gardens
Kew, Richmond
Surrey TW9 3AB

Royal Horticultural Society
80 Vincent Square
London SW1P 2PE

Rushfields of Ledbury Nursery
Ross Road
Ledbury HR8 2LP

The Savill Garden
Wick Lane, Englefield Green
Egham
Surrey SL4 2HT

Scottish Rock Garden Society
1 Hillcrest Road
Bearsden,
Glasgow G61 2EB

Sewell's Sweet Peas
81 Willingham Road
Over
Cambridge CB4 5PF

Wakefield Tulip Society
70 Wrenthorpe Lane
Wrenthorpe, Wakefield
West Yorkshire WF2 0PT

Woodfield Bros. Lupin Nursery
Wood End, Clifford Chambers
Stratford upon Avon
CV37 8HR

ACKNOWLEDGEMENTS

Bill Chudziak would like to thank the following for the help and advice they have given: Peter Buckley, Ian Cameron, Dr. James Cobb, Simon Croson, Miss Valerie Finnis VMH, Mike Hirst, Jill Hollis, Les Newby, Dr. Evelyn Stevens, and Michael Wickenden. And my greatest debt is to Janet Wheatcroft; in writing for this book, as in planning the garden at Craigieburn, we have worked together.

Jo Readman would like to thank all at Hart Ryan Productions, the contributors to the book and series, her husband Dave and children Jake and Charlie for their patience and support, and everyone out there on the gardening grapevine (they know who they are!)

Anne Swithinbank would like to thank the following – Hart Ryan Productions for making the filming of *Bloom* so enjoyable, particularly the thorough research which lead us to first-rate blooms, gardeners and gardens. I thank my husband John Swithinbank for his support and advice, as well as Liz Dean and Sue Metcalfe-Megginson from Collins and Brown for their patience and diligence.

Published by Collins & Brown Limited
London House
Great Eastern Wharf
Parkgate Road
London SW11 4NQ

Published in association with Channel Four Television Corporation and based on the series produced for Channel Four Television by Hart Ryan Productions Limited.

1 3 5 7 9 8 6 4 2

British Library Cataloguing-in-Publication Data:
A catalogue record for this title is available from the British Library.

ISBN 185585 406 6

Conceived, edited and designed by
COLLINS & BROWN LIMITED

Editorial Director: Sarah Hoggett
Senior Editor: Liz Dean
Copy Editor: Jo Weeks
Art Director: Roger Bristow
Designer: Suzanne Metcalfe-Megginson
All photography by Christopher Smith except that on page 17
(Garden Picture Library) and page172 (Clive Nichols)

Colour separation by Grafiscan, Verona
Printed in Great Britain by Butler & Tanner, Frome